Gimme Some Sugar

90 Devotions to Sweeten Your Day in a Godly Way

LINDA KOZAR

BroadStreet
PUBLISHING

BroadStreet Publishing® Group, LLC
Savage, Minnesota, USA
BroadStreetPublishing.com

Gimme Some Sugar: 90 Devotions to Sweeten Your Day in a Godly Way
Copyright © 2024 Linda Kozar

9781424567386 (faux leather)
9781424567393 (ebook)

Cover and interior by Garborg Design Works | garborgdesign.com

Printed in China

24 25 26 27 28 5 4 3 2 1

Sending some sugar to
my ninety-one-year-old
mother, Mama Rose,
who gave all the hugs
and kisses this spunky
southern child ever
needed and more.

Introduction

When I was growing up, greetings in our big southern family always involved a warm hug and a kiss on the cheek or the top of the head. The big kiss on the cheek left either a red lip imprint or a sloppy frosted-pink one, depending on whether your grandma or one of your aunts gave you some sugar. Knee babies didn't seem to mind all the cooing and affection, but older kids shied away from the mushy stuff. Until they grew up and started to do likewise.

Looking back, all those frequent, genuine expressions of love and affection in my life taught me the importance of letting our loved ones know just how much we love and care about them. Family and friends don't have to ask me to give them some sugar—I'm gonna insist!

Gimme Some Sugar is written with great affection for all of you. Be blessed!

The older I get,
the more I understand
why roosters just scream
to start their day.

Pray or Be Prey

"In this world you will have trouble.
But take heart! I have overcome the world."
JOHN 16:33 NIV

Foghorn Leghorn, the animated rooster in the ever-popular Looney Tunes and Merrie Melodies cartoons, is a fictional character, but don't try to tell him that. In his world, he fancies himself the ruler of the roost. But Foghorn is forever plagued by the other characters in the barnyard. George P. Dog (a.k.a. Barnyard Dawg), his archenemy, and Henery Hawk, the tiny, tough-guy chicken hawk, are constantly hunting him down. "Nice boy," Foghorn says of Henery, "but he's got more nerve than a bum tooth."[1] And Miss Prissy, the skinny, bespeckled spinster hen, is always chasing after his affections, although he says, "Gal reminds me of a highway between Forth Worth and Dallas—no curves."[2]

Because of Barnyard Dawg, Henery Hawk, and husband-hunting Miss Prissy, Foghorn has to sleep with one eye open.

SWEET SPOONFUL

Like Foghorn Leghorn, you may be surrounded by opposition, stress, and downright chaos while you're busy trying to do your job. But you have a friend in Jesus, who is looking out for you (John 15:15). Trust in him instead of your own strength and abilities, and he will help you overcome whatever "foul" situations you may find yourself in.

I can't wait
for the day
when I don't
have to miss you
anymore.

Family Reunion

"He will wipe away every tear from their eyes."
REVELATION 21:4 AMP

The great Southern Baptist preacher Hyman Appelman once told a story about a train engineer whose home was near the tracks. Each day when he passed, the engineer would toot the engine's whistle to the delight of his six-year-old daughter. She would poke her head and shoulders through a hole in the fence to wave at him.

But the child came down with double pneumonia, and the family doctor told the engineer and his wife what no parent wants to hear. When the girl saw their tears, she asked her parents why they were crying. The doctor took her hand and told her that her parents were sad because she was leaving them to go be with Jesus.

"Daddy, Mamma, don't cry," the little girl said. "When I get to heaven, the first thing I am going to do is tell Jesus about you. I am going to tell Him what a good Daddy and Mamma you were and how you always talked to me about Him. Then I am going to ask Jesus to take a board out of the wall around heaven. Every day I shall go to that opening and watch for you. When I see you coming, I shall wave at you to show you where I am that you may come to me."[3]

SWEET SPOONFUL

A great and glorious reunion awaits us in heaven. We will be united with those we have lost, and we will never again be separated, for the only tears in heaven are tears of joy.

I learned my first rule
about barbecue that day.
You don't put
cole slaw on it.
I think that's in
Deuteronomy somewhere.

–Lewis Grizzard

Cue the BBQ

"Every moving thing that lives shall be food for you.
And as I gave you the green plants, I give you everything."
GENESIS 9:3 ESV

There are four important food groups for those who live in southern climes: fried chicken, biscuits and gravy, banana pudding, and barbecue. Barbecue is unique in the grouping because it is both a noun and a verb. Some people say there are four main types of barbecue: beef, pork, chicken, and roadkill.

But all kidding aside, people both north and south of the Mason-Dixon Line are picky about their barbecue. There are Kansas City, Memphis, Carolina, Texas 'cues, and many other variations. And no matter what anyone tries to tell you different, they're all finger-licking good. Everyone knows that after you're finished eating ribs and sausage and chicken and pork and turkey and whatever else they served at the backyard 'cue, you're going to look like an extra in a zombie movie. Nobody cares about that though.

SWEET SPOONFUL

God created us to do life together, to experience memorable times with one another, to pray and care for one another, and to be good influences in each other's lives. We are to love God and love one another (John 13:34). If you're rusty at entertaining, a backyard barbecue is a good way to start. Don't let anyone tell you different—any get-together with those you love and care about is the best sauce.

In my defense,
I was left
unsupervised.

A House Divided

When the LORD finished speaking to Moses on Mount Sinai,
he gave him the two tablets of the covenant law,
the tablets of stone inscribed by the finger of God.

EXODUS 31:18 NIV

While the Israelites frolicked pagan-like around a golden
calf they'd fashioned with Egyptian gold, Moses made his
way slowly down Mount Sinai. With the brightness of God's
shekinah glory still shining from Moses' face, he carried the
Ten Commandments of God in his arms. But the people were
too busy worshiping a false idol to notice (Exodus 32:1–20).

What a shocking sight that must have been! The
Israelites had grown impatient for Moses' return, so they
abandoned God for an idol, a rebellious act of apostasy from
people who had seen God part the sea for them, God's cloud
by day and pillar of fire by night, and all the other miracles
God had done for them. Serving a false god was the ultimate
in-your-face rejection of the Lord.

SWEET SPOONFUL

When Moses caught his people in red-handed rebellion,
he acted quickly, separating the sheep from the goats, so to
speak. And Jesus will do the same when he returns to the
earth on the Mount of Olives. He will separate us, some
to their eternal reward in heaven and others to eternal
perdition in hell. If you are tempted to give up hope of
Christ's return and go after an idol, remember that God
always keeps his Word even when we don't.

Those that will not fear
the eternal God,
he can make afraid
of a shadow.

–Matthew Henry

Unspoken

Jonathan said to his armor-bearer, "Come up after me,
for the LORD has given them into the hand of Israel."
1 SAMUEL 14:12 ESV

A massive Philistine army encamped nearby ready to
obliterate the small, dwindling army of men Jonathan and
his disobedient father, Saul, had with them. Instead of
staying put, Jonathan with just his armor-bearer set off to
the enemy garrison to fight, saying, "Nothing can hinder
the LORD from saving by many or by few" (v. 6). Why did
Jonathan take such a great risk against such a great enemy?

Some say he acted on divine impulse, trusting God
to lead him as in Psalm 32:8: "I will instruct you and teach
you in the way you should go." Jonathan told his servant that
if the enemy called to them to go up to fight, they would.
The Philistines did exactly that. And the two men climbed
up the rocks and dispatched all twenty of the soldiers. Then
suddenly the earth began to quake! Terror and panic ensued.
The Philistines had all the earthly advantages, but they were
defeated because they did not have God.

SWEET SPOONFUL

Whatever trouble you find yourself in, if you acknowledge
the Lord, walk in obedience, and seek him in all your ways,
you have nothing to fear. The odds may be stacked against
you, but if you side with him, you have all you need. In fact,
if you have God, you have everything.

My wife's idea of
housecleaning is
to sweep the room
with a glance.

–Joey Adams

Next to Godliness

"When it comes, it finds the house swept and put in order."
LUKE 11:25 ESV

If your idea of cleaning is putting stuff in less obvious places, there's a good chance you're shabby without the chic. To determine if you have a messy home, this is what happens when you find out an unexpected visitor is five minutes away: Your kids are highly trained mess-hider ninjas. They dash into a mad scramble, stuffing what's on the floor under couches and beds. You throw dirty dishes willy-nilly into the dishwasher. You jam into the back of your van a pile of clean laundry that has been begging for a fold. You stuff stacks of papers and food wrappers and pizza boxes into garbage bags to sort through later. Much later.

You apologize to your guest. "The house is usually clean." But your guest knows you're fudging the truth— because you can't hide the peanut butter smeared all over the cabinets, a bathtub so dirty you have to wear flip-flops to take a shower, and the cat box overflowing. If your decorating style is best described as "there appears to have been a struggle," maybe it's time for a change.

SWEET SPOONFUL

The truth is that it takes as much energy to hide messes as to clean them up. Keeping a clean house is as difficult as living a sanctified life before God. We can't hide our misses, our messes, or our sins from our loving God, who forgives us when we come clean.

The woman at the well
came with a thirsty soul
and quenched her thirst
once and for all from
the fountain of
living water.

The Well Woman

"Sir, give me this water, so that I will not be thirsty
or have to come here to draw water."

JOHN 4:15 ESV

Jesus went out of his way to meet a certain woman at a well
in Samaria. She came alone in the heat of the day because
she was an outcast, even by loosey-goosey Samaritan
standards. Jesus asked her for a drink of water, but before she
could get over her surprise that a Jewish man would speak to
her, Jesus told her that if she asked, he would give her living
water to drink, and she would never be thirsty again.

Her jaw unhinged once more when the stranger
shared what he knew about her, especially the part about
being married five times and her current living situation. She
figured Jesus for a prophet and, when the two began to talk
about worship, told Jesus she believed in the coming Messiah
and that when he showed up, he would explain things. But
Jesus said to her, "I who speak to you am he" (v. 26). The
shame and rejection the woman had suffered for most of her
life poured out, and she was filled with joy.

SWEET SPOONFUL

The woman who walked alone with an empty waterpot to
Jacob's well left with a full heart as she ran to town to share
the good news of the Messiah. Are you suffering shame or
rejection? Jesus hears the cry of your heart and will meet you
at your well.

When you see
that sunset or that
panoramic view of God's
finest expressed in
nature, and the beauty
just takes your breath
away, remember it is
just a glimpse of
the real thing that
awaits you in heaven.

–Greg Laurie

Eclipse of the Heart

If we walk in the light, as he is in the light,
we have fellowship with one another,
and the blood of Jesus his Son cleanses us from all sin.

1 JOHN 1:7 ESV

An eclipse of the heart can happen when you least expect it. Something awful happens, and the secure world you know is gone, replaced by chilling fear and uncertainty. Sorrow and pain cover your heart like a dark shroud. An eclipse changes our world and temporarily changes the way we see things. During a solar eclipse, gaps between tree leaves become natural pinhole cameras. Usually the shadows cast on the ground by the light of the sun are round, but during an eclipse, the shadows are crescent shaped, the very image of the eclipse.

When everything looks different and is different from the normal we're used to, it seems impossible to navigate our way out of the situation we're in. But God is our light in the darkness. He loves you and will comfort and encourage you through your darkest hour. The good thing about eclipses is that they are temporary celestial events with a beginning and an end. Eclipses of the heart are like that as well. Darkness will pass.

SWEET SPOONFUL

When darkness casts a shadow over your life, call upon the Lord in the gloom of your situation. He will illuminate your path, and the darkness will not overcome you (John 1:5).

My unknown future
is in the hands of
the all-knowing God.

Fig Tree Faith

Even before a word is on my tongue,
behold, O LORD, you know it altogether.
PSALM 139:4 ESV

When Jesus saw Nathaniel approaching, Jesus said, "Here truly is an Israelite in whom there is no deceit" (John 1:47 NIV). Nathaniel had never met Jesus, so he asked him how he knew who he was. Jesus replied, "I saw you while you were still under the fig tree" (v. 48). Fig tree branches hang low to the ground. Nathaniel knew that no one else in the world could have seen that he was the "chap under the sap" of that tree.

We live in a world where our personal data is tracked via social media and shared with strangers without our knowledge or consent. Some businesses and health organizations and governments want to know everything about us, from our buying habits to what we eat and how much, from our exercise routines to what our opinions are about politics, freedom of expression, and more. The world is very interested in people but only for what it can get out of us or use to control and manipulate us.

SWEET SPOONFUL

If you knew everything about someone, everything they've done or thought about doing, the good, the bad, and the ugly, you'd shake your finger and recite the old Monopoly card, "Go to jail. Go directly to jail. Do not pass go. Do not collect $200." But Jesus loves us so much that he gave his life for us so that we could be with him for all eternity.

Ain't no way
God told Noah to
put two stink bugs
on the ark.

Bonkers about Bugs

"All winged insects that go on all fours are detestable to you."
LEVITICUS 11:20 ESV

It is a well-known fact that southerners talk to bugs before killing them. They say things like, "You done flew up in the wrong house today," or "Die, roach! You're fixing to get mashed." Do the insects understand? More importantly, do they really need to? Yet the warnings persist.

Some folks have a proper plastic swatter on hand with which to dispatch pests. Other folks utilize rolled-up newspapers or magazines. Spatulas. The heel of a boot. A kitchen towel. Some women prefer a good ol' can of Raid. And they spray a pool of insecticide on the one little creepy-crawly like they spray their hair with Aqua Net. Others deploy coils of flypaper hanging from the ceiling, a sort of bug tinsel that might be mistaken for holiday decor were it not for the summer sun. Fancy families own electric bug zappers, and we can all agree that there's nothing fancier than munching corn on the cob to the tune of exploding bugs.

SWEET SPOONFUL

Why do we get all womper-jawed when it comes to insects? A cricket's chirps keep us up at night. Mosquitoes slurp our blood and whine into our ears while we're trying to sleep. Roaches gross us out. God created these, yet he also created butterflies, honeybees, and ladybugs. God in his wisdom created all things for his plan and purpose. But we can sure pray about those other bugs.

I'm a terrible
ventriloquist,
if I do say
so myself.

Here I Am

The word of the LORD was rare and precious in those days; visions [that is, new revelations of divine truth] were not widespread.

1 SAMUEL 3:1 AMP

The idea that the God of the universe would actually speak to us goes against logical thought, yet he does. For some, it's easier to convince ourselves that we're imagining things.

Think about the many ways in which we communicate with one another. By phone, text, emails, letters, satellite, code, and carrier pigeon. But the Holy Spirit teaches and witnesses to our hearts. God speaks to us through people and situations, and he communicates peace to our hearts after we send up desperate flare prayers. God supernaturally communicates with us by any means or manner he chooses.

SWEET SPOONFUL

As a child in the temple of God, the prophet Samuel woke from a sound sleep three times to a voice calling his name. He thought the voice was that of his mentor, Eli the high priest, but the priest told the boy that the next time the voice summoned, he was to say, "Speak, for Your servant is listening" (1 Samuel 3:10). Samuel heard from God in the days when hardly anyone else did. If you long to hear from God, converse with him in prayer. Be acquainted with the Lord through his Word. And wait in faith with patience, perseverance, and praise.

A man who wants to
lead the orchestra
must turn his back
on the crowd.

–Max Lucado

Pilate's Wife

While he was seated on the judgment seat, his wife sent him a message, saying, "Have nothing to do with that righteous and innocent Man; for last night I suffered greatly in a dream because of Him."

MATTHEW 27:19 AMP

Little is known about the wife of the infamous Pontius Pilate, the Roman governor of Judea. But the book of Matthew mentions that she desperately pleaded with her husband. God had sent a dream to warn her about an eternally unrighteous judgment her husband was about to make. The dream bothered her so much that she sent word to Pilate as he sat on the judge's bench.

But Pilate was already wondering why the Jews had brought this man called Jesus before him. In his gut, he knew the man was innocent, yet the chief priests and elders had already persuaded the crowd to go against Jesus. They called instead for Barabbas, the zealot terrorist and murderer, to be set free. So Pilate ignored his wife's dire warning and sentenced Jesus to be crucified. He washed his hands of the blood of Jesus, proclaiming his own innocence. But only the blood of Jesus could wash Pilate's sins away.

SWEET SPOONFUL

Pilate listened to the voice of the multitudes when he should have listened to God. He chose popularity over principle. We should always listen to the voice of the one true God over the worldly multitude of voices urged on by the Enemy.

Be ye fishers of men.
You catch them;
he'll clean them.

Fish Tales

Simon answering said unto him, Master,
we have toiled all the night, and have taken nothing:
nevertheless at thy word I will let down the net.

LUKE 5:5 KJV

When you go fishing for fun and don't catch anything, it's no big deal. But when you're fishing to feed your family and catch zip, you might very well go hungry. Simon Peter and his partners, James and John, were cleaning their nets of smelly stuff after an exhausting and unproductive night of fishing when Jesus suddenly stepped into Peter's boat to preach. When he was finished preaching, Jesus told Peter to launch out into the deep and let down his nets.

Now, Simon Peter knew that Jesus was no fisherman, and he certainly knew that fishing with a net was best done at night. Besides that, the noisy crowds listening to Jesus preach had probably scared away any scant number of fish there were. But Peter obeyed. And to his amazement, they pulled in so many fish that the nets started breaking and the boat started sinking under the weight.

SWEET SPOONFUL

What can we learn from this? Your past failures do not determine your future successes. Simon Peter believed in Jesus, not in the circumstance, and he hauled in the catch of a lifetime. And his life would never be the same, for he would soon become a fisher of men.

I intend to
live forever or
die trying.

–Groucho Marx

In the End

"Truly, truly, I say to you, whoever hears my word and
believes him who sent me has eternal life. He does not come
into judgment, but has passed from death to life."

JOHN 5:24 ESV

Some people take their sense of humor to the grave with
them, literally. For example, John Yeast's epitaph reads,
"Pardon me for not rising," and the tombstone of Mel Blanc,
who voiced the Bugs Bunny cartoons and is known as the
"Man of a Thousand Voices," is carved with just three words:
"That's all, folks."[8]

Ruth McCue Bell Graham, the wife of well-known
evangelist Billy Graham, decided to go a different route in
selecting her own epitaph. She was driving home one day
and had to pass through a stretch of road construction, with
detours and lots of warning signs. When she came to the final
sign, she laughed when she read it: "End of construction.
Thank you for your patience." She later told her family that
she wanted that particular message on her gravestone, and
she wrote it down for them so they wouldn't forget.[9]

When we come to the end of our lives and arrive
home, we will look back at all the work God has done on us
and thank him for his patience.

SWEET SPOONFUL

Though we sometimes take a wrong turn, the highway to
heaven is the road to a right life with Christ.

The Bible says a great deal about entire families coming to Christ...Rahab the harlot...the Philippian jailer...Cornelius, the Roman centurion...You may be the one who could lead your family to Christ.

—Billy Graham

Rahab Rehab

"When we heard of it, our hearts melted in fear and everyone's courage failed because of you, for the LORD your God is God in heaven above and on the earth below."

JOSHUA 2:11 NIV

Rahab was a Canaanite woman who lived in a walled city you might have heard about in Sunday School when you sang, "Joshua fought the battle of Jericho, Jericho, Jericho..." Rahab might have been employed as a prostitute or simply had an inn with a house of ill repute attached. Either way, Scripture refers to her as Rahab the harlot. Not a good moniker.

Rahab's whole family lived with her in a house that was built into the city wall. Joshua sent spies into the city to reconnoiter, but they were spotted and sought refuge in Rahab's place. She hid the men under bunches of flax on the roof and told them that the fear of God was upon all Jericho. Rahab asked them for mercy in exchange for risking her life to save them. They agreed and told her to hang a red cord out of her window so that she and her family would be spared. Some say the red cord is symbolic of the blood of Jesus.

SWEET SPOONFUL

God called Rahab to leave her old life behind, to serve him, and to be a blessing for all eternity. Perhaps the flax from which priestly linen is made offers a prophetic bread crumb to the High Priest in the order of Melchizedek who would come through Rahab's lineage: Jesus.

The devil drives
his hogs to
a bad market.

–Charles Spurgeon

When Pigs Fly

Behold, they cried out, saying,
What have we to do with thee, Jesus, thou Son of God?
art thou come hither to torment us before the time?
MATTHEW 8:29 KJV

Maybe you've read in Mark or Luke about the "Demoniac of Gergesenes," the crazed demon-possessed guy who lived among the tombs. But Matthew mentions that not one but two men possessed by demons came out to meet Jesus. A demonic duo. Why the discrepancy?

Augustine suggested that there were indeed two demoniacs but that one was more well-known and that the severity of his possession made the miracle even more amazing. That man was possessed by a legion of six thousand demons. Maybe the other guy was still in training. The demons wanted Jesus to leave them alone and asked if Jesus had come to torment them before their time. The spirits recognized exactly who Jesus was, and they referenced the everlasting torment that awaits them in the final judgment.

SWEET SPOONFUL

Jesus saw what these demons had done to the two men. They lived among the tombs in utter filth and want, separated from family, friends, and God. Jesus cast the demons out of the men and into a herd of swine that promptly stampeded over a cliff. The men were set free.

When is the first mention
of insurance in the Bible?
When Adam and Eve
needed coverage.

Exit This Way

"You must not eat from the tree of the knowledge of good and evil, for when you eat from it you will certainly die."
GENESIS 2:17 NIV

The moment that Adam and Eve ate the forbidden fruit from the Tree of Knowledge of Good and Evil, they saw that they were naked. So the two clothing rookies cobbled together loincloths from sticky, sappy, prickly fig leaves. Maybe they should have tried using banana leaves instead.

We tend to think of the garden of Eden as a pristine and perfect place, but Eden was not secure from evil. The serpent was also in the garden (Ezekiel 28:13), and he tempted Adam and Eve to disobey God and eat the fruit from the forbidden tree. Before they sinned, it is likely that Adam and Eve were clothed in the light of God's glory (Psalm 104:2). In the absence of his light, Adam and Eve saw themselves without God's covering, and they were ashamed. Adam and Eve started out well until sin darkened their lives.

SWEET SPOONFUL

How Satan must have smirked when God's children were cast out of the paradise of Eden just as God had cast Satan out of heaven. Though we are born into the darkness of sin, God made a way of redemption through the blood of his own Son. When we open our hearts to Jesus Christ, our eyes are opened to his holy light, and we are clothed in his righteousness.

Love was
in the air
till Delilah
cut his hair.

The Great Hair-After

I can do all this through him who gives me strength.
PHILIPPIANS 4:13 NIV

There are two guys in the Bible known for their great heads of hair, Samson and Absalom—the hair dudes. A Nazarite from his miraculous birth (Judges 13), Samson didn't spend a moment hulking up in the gym. Shaggy Samson's long mane of manly hair was the secret of his strength. Though he was a righteous judge in Israel for twenty years, Samson had moral weaknesses, one of which was an eye for the ladies.

As for Absalom, it was said that there was not a single flaw from the sole of his foot to the top of his head, which by the way, was framed in long, luxurious hair (2 Samuel 14:25–26). His prissy palace kid flaws were on the inside: pride, vanity, cunning ambition, betrayal, and disloyalty.

SWEET SPOONFUL

Absalom led others to join him in rebellion against his own father and died, ironically, due to his long, luscious hair, which caught in the branches of a tree as he was retreating on his mule. He kicked his legs in vain, caught between heaven and earth.

Samson dallied with a woman named Delilah. Bribed by the promise of silver, she nagged him for the secret of his strength, which he foolishly revealed. Shaved, blinded, and enslaved by the Philistines, Samson asked God to give him avenging strength, and he brought down the house on the Philistines, dying a hero of the Bible.

I've lived so long
that my friends
in heaven are
going to think
I didn't make it.

Lamb's Book

Another book was opened, which is the book of life.
And the dead were judged by what was written in the books,
according to what they had done.

REVELATION 20:12 ESV

Have you ever thought about writing down your life story
or personal testimony? In the United States of America
alone, over two hundred million people have expressed the
desire to publish a book.[11] Now, should everyone publish a
book? Probably not. Though it is easy enough these days to
independently publish, there is no guarantee that anyone
would actually want to read your book. Though we are not
all writers, we all have a story to tell.

A memoir is a collection of private memories
someone shares about their life experiences. These personal
memories usually reveal something important about the
person or offer a universal message. A Christian testimony
is the story behind not only your come-to-Jesus moment
but also your life, and life after the altar call is when things
truly get interesting. Your testimony is your superpower as a
believer (Revelation 12:11).

SWEET SPOONFUL

There is a story behind the name of every person in the Lamb's
Book of Life. Some stories we have yet to hear, of heroism and
suffering, of courage and self-sacrifice, of kindness and love.
One day we will hear the testimonies of all the saints, of all
believers who loved and are the beloved of God.

Hardships often
prepare people
for an
extraordinary
destiny.

–Reepicheep,
Voyage of the Dawn Treader (2010 film)

Spare

When Athaliah the mother of Ahaziah saw that her son was
dead, she arose and destroyed all the royal heirs.

2 KINGS 11:1 NKJV

The award for the worst grandmother of all time has got to
go to Baal-worshiping Queen Athaliah. You can read about
her in 2 Kings 8–11. The daughter of King Ahab and Queen
Jezebel, Athaliah married Jehoram, king of Judah, to seal a
treaty. Jehoram was succeeded by their son, King Ahaziah,
who was assassinated after only one year. The new king of
Israel had Athaliah's entire family in Samaria put to death. So
she seized the throne and wiped out her own grandchildren
to destroy all descendants to the house of David in Judah.

However, Jehosheba, Ahaziah's half sister, hid one-
year-old Joash in a room where spare furniture was kept.
Jehosheba was married to a priest named Jehoiada, and
they raised the boy in the temple for six years until Jehoiada
gathered faithful military leaders and put Athaliah's brief
reign as the one and only queen of Judah to an end.

SWEET SPOONFUL

God kept his promise to David that he would establish the
throne of his kingdom forever (2 Samuel 7:12–13). The little
king, hidden at first in a closet full of spare items, was the
last soul spared of the house of David. When your situation
seems hopeless, trust in God instead of your circumstance.
Be confident that God always keeps his promises.

Our days are happier
when we give people
a piece of our heart
rather than a
piece of our mind.

Golden Rule

"Whatever you wish that others would do to you,
do also to them, for this is the Law and the Prophets."
MATTHEW 7:12 ESV

"School days, school days. Dear old Golden Rule days…"
Once a popular tune, "School Days," written in 1907, is
about a mature married couple's sentimental look back on
their childhood together in primary school. The sweet song
was sung by schoolchildren in the classroom and played on
many a piano at home.

Back in those days, children learned to write the
Golden Rule on slate tablets, but over the years, the majority
of Americans have forgotten or never learned these wise
words. The Golden Rule is described by some as a maxim,
but what might be a maxim to some is a scriptural command
to believers. In the Golden Rule, Jesus tells us to treat others
as we would like to be treated (Matthew 7:12), and in Mark
12:31, the Lord commands, "You shall love your neighbor as
yourself."

SWEET SPOONFUL

One characteristic that most of us share is that we're always
looking out for our own best interest. When you confess
your sins, Jesus wipes the slate clean. Instead of a "treat
yourself" attitude, why not treat others the way you want to
be treated? The Golden Rule is a measure of your character
that can only be measured by our "Ruler."

You may be an
undigested bit of beef...
a fragment of underdone
potato. There's more of
gravy than of grave about
you, whatever you are!

–Charles Dickens,
A Christmas Carol

That Wasn't Chicken

Be kind to one another, tenderhearted, forgiving one
another, as God in Christ forgave you.

EPHESIANS 4:32 ESV

Food poisoning is an equal opportunity stomach bug. Not
long after eating off-temp "tacos of terror" or "chicken
dia-blow" overrun with bacteria, you suddenly feel like
porcupines are doing pirouettes in your stomach. Whatever
food happened to be the culprit will be on your no-go list
for an indefinite period of time. We tend to blame the food,
not the microscopic fiend that took advantage of a dirty
restaurant kitchen.

Have you ever been hurt by a fellow believer? You
never expect to be wounded by another Christian. That's
why it hurts all the more. Our instinct is to draw away from
others to protect ourselves from being hurt again. Or we
blame the whole thing on God. But should we turn our back
on God based on what a brother or sister in Christ did to us?

SWEET SPOONFUL

As you recover from food poisoning, your body feels as
wrung out as a used tea bag, but eventually your stomach
will growl again. And as you recover emotionally from
betrayal, insults, and wounds from others, you will hunger
for fellowship and put your heart on the line again. Some
people will hurt you, and some people will love you. As
Frederick William Robertson said, "We win by tenderness.
We conquer by forgiveness."[13]

One of two things you
must do; you must either
receive Him or reject Him.
You receive Him here, and
He will receive you there;
you reject Him here and
He will reject you there.

–Dwight L. Moody

23

Sink or Swim

Deep calls to deep at the roar of your waterfalls;
all your breakers and your waves have gone over me.
PSALM 42:7 ESV

Have you ever wanted to change something in the past or look around the corner and see your future? If you could, you might be able to avoid making foolish mistakes and bad decisions. With true knowledge of your destiny before you, decisions would be a no-brainer, right? Yet God has given us a crystal clear picture of what's ahead for believers and unbelievers.

God freely shares his wisdom with us. His Word is true, and his promises to us, as well as warnings of events to come, are in the book of Revelation. God gives each of us free will to choose to live in joyful eternity with him or to choose a bleak, hopeless eternity without him.

SWEET SPOONFUL

Evangelist Vance Havner once said,

> I remember when the Titanic sank in 1912, it was
> the ship that was supposed to be unsinkable. The
> only thing it ever did was sink. When it took off
> from England, all kinds of passengers were aboard—
> millionaires, celebrities, people of moderate means,
> and poor folks down in the steerage. But a few hours
> later when they put the list in the Cunard office in
> New York, it carried only two categories—lost and
> saved. Grim tragedy had leveled all distinctions.[14]

Most of us can
keep a secret.
It's the people
we tell it to
who can't.

24

Mum's the Word

All kinds of animals, birds, reptiles and sea creatures are
being tamed and have been tamed by mankind,
but no human being can tame the tongue.
It is a restless evil, full of deadly poison.

JAMES 3:7–8 NIV

Keeping secrets is hard. And for some of us, keeping
even one secret is pretty near impossible. You might tell
a friend, "Your secret is safe with me," but your tongue is
already chomping at the bit. Benjamin Franklin once said
of discretion, "Three may keep a secret if two of them are
dead." The desire to betray can be stronger than the smell of
an acre of garlic. Holding that classified information inside is
a monumental task.

In the Bible, James 3:3 talks about putting bits into
horses' mouths so the horses will obey the rider and turn
in the direction their rider wishes. Anyone who can master
their own tongue has control over their whole body (v. 2).
Our tongue is the most difficult muscle to give orders to, but
if you don't control your tongue, something else will.

SWEET SPOONFUL

Letting the cat out of the bag is a whole lot easier than
putting it back in. Revealing a secret breaks trust and can
ruin a friendship. "He who is trustworthy in spirit keeps
a thing covered" (Proverbs 11:13 ESV). Self-discipline
develops greatness of character. But to be thought of as
trustworthy, one has to be worthy of trust.

You never have to advertise a fire. You don't have to advertise it in the newspaper, forget it. You let the glory of the Lord fill the temple; people will come from hundreds of miles.

–Leonard Ravenhill

25

Revival!

"'In the last days it shall be, God declares, that I will pour out my Spirit on all flesh, and your sons and your daughters shall prophesy, and your young men shall see visions, and your old men shall dream dreams.'"

ACTS 2:17 ESV

Many Christians are hoping and praying for a great revival of God to come. Some churches pitch their tents in hopes of kick-starting a revival of passionate renewal toward God. Others talk about revival in academic terms, wondering when God will send another movement.

But those who are serious about revival and truly desire God's fire are praying hard. They know that revival can only begin when God himself lights the modest ember to the fire of true revival. The rushing wind of the Holy Spirit (Acts 2:2) will ignite new faith in the faithless and stoke fresh flames in the hearts of believers. Jesus baptizes us with the Holy Spirit and with fire (Matthew 3:11). Have you heard the expression "Fight fire with fire"? Well, God will put out fires from hell with the hearts of those on fire with the Holy Spirit.

SWEET SPOONFUL

God is eager to pour out his Spirit on all flesh. People will be so desperate to know how to be saved that they will pull aside strangers to ask them about Jesus. Like fish jumping into the net, revival will gather the family of God from far and near. Are you ready?

Did it bother
anybody else
that the guy from
the Operation game
was clearly
wide awake?

26

Operation You

> "Every branch in Me that does not bear fruit He takes away;
> and every branch that bears fruit He prunes,
> that it may bear more fruit."
>
> JOHN 15:2 NKJV

Did you ever play the Operation game when you were a kid? You poked inside Cavity Sam with "electro probe tweezers" to pull out fanciful internal organs like a "funny bone," "butterflies in stomach," "writer's cramp," "spare ribs," and even a "broken heart." But, if you inadvertently touched the side of a small cavity, a buzzer would go off, and Sam's red nose would light up.

Like Sam, most of us carry around useless odds and ends that God wants to remove so that we can grow and prosper in him. But the Lord won't remove what we don't approve. If we are unwilling to let go of the secret things we're holding on to, the tweezer will set off our internal buzzer, and the item will fall right back into place.

SWEET SPOONFUL

No one goes into an operating room fully clothed. In order to be set free from useless bits and pieces, we must first be transparent to God. Next, we have to acknowledge the junk we're carrying around as well as the reason we've been giving it space in our lives and repent. Finally, we must allow God to clear out those sins one by one and ask him to occupy those spaces so that we can mature and fulfill our calling in him.

God, when he pleases,
can make the worst
of places serve
the best purposes.

–Matthew Henry

27

Drink Up

If I forget you, O Jerusalem, let my right hand forget its skill!
If I do not remember you, let my tongue cling to the roof of
my mouth—if I do not exalt Jerusalem above my chief joy.

PSALM 137:5–6 NKJV

Nehemiah lived life on the edge. Or more on the rim.
Among his other important duties, he was the cupbearer to
King Artaxerxes, the sixth king of the Medo-Persian Empire.
Poison was one of the modi operandi of the king's enemies.
The next sip of vintage wine might be the cupbearer's last.
But aside from that, Nehemiah made good bank, lived in the
palace citadel, and was held in high esteem by the king. But
he was in exile from his homeland, Jerusalem.

One day, when some brethren from Judah came to the
citadel, Nehemiah asked them about the state of Jerusalem.
When they told him that the city's walls were all broken
down and its gates burned with fire, his heart was greatly
distressed. In ancient times, a city without walls was like a
house without walls, vulnerable and unsafe from its enemies.

SWEET SPOONFUL

For months, Nehemiah fasted and prayed, wept and mourned,
so much so that the king noticed. He poured his heart out
to the king, who decided to help him. He gave Nehemiah
whatever he asked for to rebuild the walls of Jerusalem, and
the king released him to do the work God had called him to
do. God breached the walls of Nehemiah's heart before he
could use his servant to repair the walls of Jerusalem.

All heroes are
shadows of Christ.

-John Piper

28

Count It All Joy

Rejoice and exult in hope; be steadfast and patient in
suffering and tribulation; be constant in prayer.

ROMANS 12:12 AMPC

Have you heard the expression "caught between a rock and a
hard place"? When you find yourself smack dab in the middle
of trouble, go ahead and drop a GPS pin—you're there.

The residents of the remote Derbyshire village of
Eyam in England were faced with such a dilemma when they
suffered an outbreak of bubonic plague in the year 1665.
The plague began when a young tailor's assistant opened a
package from plague-ravished London. The bag of cloth was
infested with fleas, and the disease spread rapidly. A newly
appointed rector, William Mompesson, knew that the only
solution was to establish a cordon sanitaire, quarantine, to
keep the plague from spreading outside the small town. At
its peak, the plague took five or six lives per day. One woman
saw six of her children and her husband die on the family
farm in a span of just eight days.[17]

SWEET SPOONFUL

The rector's wife, Catherine, tended to the sick at his side
but died near the end of the outbreak in August 1666.
Mompesson survived. In the end, the plague claimed
260 lives in Eyam but did not spread to neighboring
communities. Though they could not change their situation,
they decided to protect others from the same sad fate.

Even in the poorest neighborhoods you can find a geranium in a coffee can, a window box set against the scaling side of a tenement, a border of roses struggling to live in a tiny patch of open ground. Where flowers bloom, so does hope.

–Lady Bird Johnson

29

Flower Fields

"All flesh is like grass and all its glory like the flower of grass.
The grass withers, and the flower falls."
1 PETER 1:24 ESV

Some people can look at a field or meadow blooming with
wildflowers and see the glory of God while others only see only
weeds. Before her husband became president, Lady Bird
Johnson gently campaigned for him across Texas by speaking
to garden clubs. The clubs aimed to beautify highways and
byways with a colorful palette of wildflowers. The meetings
would conclude with caravans of ladies flinging wildflower
seeds from their car windows along country roads.

After Lyndon B. Johnson became president, he put the
federal government behind his wife's work with the Highway
Beautification Act of 1965, and she took her beautification
and conservation efforts nationwide. With fragrant
bluebonnets and the evening primrose in Texas, black-eyed
Susans throughout North America, and white glacier lilies
in Washington state, the roadside views across America
suddenly transformed from somber stretches of highway to
scenic destinations.[19]

SWEET SPOONFUL

You, too, can make a difference in this world by bringing
brightness to barren places, planting seeds of the gospel, and
sharing the salvation message of blessed hope with others.

I told my dentist my
teeth are going yellow.
He told me to wear
a brown necktie.

—Rodney Dangerfield,
comedian

30

You Know the Drill

Your teeth are like a flock of shorn ewes that have come
up from the washing, all of which bear twins, and not one
among them has lost its young.
SONG OF SOLOMON 4:2 ESV

The calendar on your phone sets off a little alarm, and you
stop in your tracks to read the reminder. Dentist tomorrow.
Ack! Your dentist can be sweet as pie to your face, but the
moment he or she breaks out that grindy drill and the hooks
and picks and whatnots of whatever medieval torture devices
are lying on that steel tray, you won't look at your dentist the
same way. Whether it's for a cleaning or a crown, you know
the appointment is for your own good. But you will never
look forward to your next visit.

Telling the truth to someone can be as painful as
pulling a tooth. Maybe your friend or family member is in
sin and deceived into thinking their actions or behaviors
aren't sinful. Sitting someone down to tell them the truth is
good, godly, and necessary for their spiritual health. Telling
the truth *in love* is an act of love. We want to avoid such
confrontations even though we know the end result will be
beneficial.

SWEET SPOONFUL

Long ago, before sugar-free anything existed, dentists used to
hand out lollipops to their young patients after a visit. Was it
to ensure continued business? Who knows? It sure worked.
At least the lollipop was something to look forward to.

Our willingness to wait
reveals the value we
place on the object
we're waiting for.

–Charles Stanley

31

Wait-y Matters

Abraham was a hundred years old
when his son Isaac was born to him.
GENESIS 21:5 NIV

Have you ever tried to second-guess God? You're impatient for God's response to the time-sensitive thing you've been praying for, and that answer doesn't come. We start getting antsy and maybe a little annoyed. Did God hear me? Is he too busy to help? That's when we get into trouble, imagining what we think God would do or what we think he should do for us.

Remember Abram and Sarai when they were waiting on their promise? God told Abram he would be the father of many nations before he'd even fathered a child. And Sarai was already wearing silver sneakers by that time, well past her childbearing years. She wanted to be a mommy, but her womb had turned to mummy dust. However, God can do anything, and his delays are not his denials. God turned back the clock on Abram and Sarai, now called Abraham and Sarah, and Sarah gave birth to Isaac at ninety. Who else but God could anyone ascribe this miracle to?

SWEET SPOONFUL

There are times when we've all tried to fill in the blanks for God's will and intent with our own. But God knows what we have need of before we ask. Sometimes God waits until the miracle he sends will bring the most glory or touch the hearts of the most people. Pray for a miracle and trust God's timing.

It is ordained of
old that the cross of
trouble should be
engraved on every
vessel of mercy,
as the royal mark
whereby the King's
vessels of honor
are distinguished.

–Charles Spurgeon

32

True Treasure

In a great house there are not only vessels of gold and silver
but also of wood and clay, some for honorable use,
some for dishonorable.

2 TIMOTHY 2:20 ESV

A gleaming silver tray crafted of high-quality silver, the
kind of item displayed on a royal buffet in a grand palace or
estate, almost always bears what is called a silver hallmark of
distinction. The insignia, crest, or stamp are on all items set
apart for royalty. We bear such a mark because we are royal
sons and daughters in God's kingdom (Revelation 9:4).

How many times have you heard the saying "You can't
make a silk purse out of a sow's ear"? But God can! Our spirit
comes to life eternal the moment we repent and confess to
Jesus, and the hallmark of distinction upon us is his own
precious blood. When we conform our lives to God's Word,
he transforms us from vessels of the earth to precious vessels
fit for use in his temple. When the heat is high, impurities
rise to the surface and are skimmed off. When we trust in
God, we are perfected in our most uncomfortable situations
and polished to a high gleam that reflects God's light.

SWEET SPOONFUL

Whenever you feel worthless or without value in this world,
remember that you are a precious vessel of God, the treasure
of his heart, stamped with his insignia, and fit for use in his
kingdom.

My identity is based
on belonging to God.
No one can take
this foundation
away from me.

–Tim Tebow

Shake Well before Using

The words "once more" indicate the removing
of what can be shaken—that is, created things—
so that what cannot be shaken may remain.
HEBREWS 12:27 NIV

The people who prefer to buy live trees in anticipation of the
Christmas season visit a Christmas tree farm to pick out the
perfect evergreen. After the tree is cut down, the next step is to
put it through the shaker, a handy-dandy machine that shakes
off all the loose tree needles. A house littered with sticky, sappy
needles can really take the merry out of Christmas.

At times, God shakes things up in our lives as well, all
to remove the dead leaves and branches and the unnecessary
burdens weighing us down. Sometimes we are the cause
of the extra weight. Like pack rats, we hold on to scraps of
earthly things we'll never use to further the kingdom of God
or bring him glory. So what remains after God shakes us?
First Corinthians 13:13 gives us the answer: "Three things
will last forever—faith, hope, and love—and the greatest of
these is love" (NLT).

SWEET SPOONFUL

Evangelist Dr. Vance Havner said, "Sometimes your
medicine bottle says, 'Shake well before using.' That is what
God has to do with some of his people. He has to shake
them well before they are usable."[23] If you're going through
a shaking in your life right now, look out! God might be
getting ready to use you.

Our fall has always been,
and always will be,
that we aren't satisfied in
God and what He gives.
We hunger for something
more, something other.

–Ann Voskamp

34

A Change

Like newborn babies, crave pure spiritual milk,
so that by it you may grow up in your salvation.
1 PETER 2:2 NIV

Toddlers can make diaper changes look like MMA cage fights. They're in that in-between stage when they want to be independent but still long for their mother's undivided attention. New believers, like newborn babies, start out on the milk of the Word, but at some point, they must move on to solid food. Even so, some believers never want to venture past the bottle-fed stage until they are eventually drinking watered-down skim milk, if any at all.

To grow and mature, believers need the meat of the Word. Without it, you'll end up like this: "In fact, though by this time you ought to be teachers, you need someone to teach you the elementary truths of God's word all over again" (Hebrews 5:12). God wants his children to grow and mature, to fulfill the callings on their lives and become the people of God they are meant to be.

SWEET SPOONFUL

If you're not hungry for God, you're probably full of yourself. "Taste and see that the LORD is good" (Psalm 34:8). Make a habit of reading your Bible every day. A morning read is a good practice to launch your day, but anytime of the day or night is good if it works for you. How often do you eat? How often do you crave snacks? Read your Bible and feed your hungry spirit as well as your body.

A mother's hug lasts
long after she lets go.

35

That Tender Loving Care

Whoever brings blessing will be enriched,
and one who waters will himself be watered.
PROVERBS 11:25 ESV

Years ago, if you skinned your knee, your mother would open
a bottle of mercurochrome and paint the red solution all
over your wound, which stung like the devil's spit. But it sure
worked. Now parents use an antibiotic ointment and cartoon
bandages. When you caught a cold, your mother would give
you a little pink baby aspirin. Then she'd break out the Vicks
VapoRub and plaster it all over your chest, topped with a
clean hanky or some flannel. Funny thing, when you woke up
the next morning, you almost always felt better. And let's not
forget velvety custard or chicken soup. There might not have
been anything medicinal in chicken soup, but that bowl of
goodness somehow cured whatever ailed you.

Looking back, we sometimes long for the tender
loving care we received from our mothers when we were
children. Indeed, the roles have changed. You might be
the one taking care of one or both of your parents now or
visiting them in a care facility.

SWEET SPOONFUL

There are many ways we can shower love and affection on
our loved ones. Even if your mother doesn't seem to hear or
respond, read to her, bring her pretty flowers, pray with her,
play the music she used to love. Give a big hug and kiss to
the dearest woman who once cradled you in her arms.

"Do not touch"
must be one of the
scariest things
to read in Braille.

36

The Human Touch

Greet one another with a holy kiss.

2 CORINTHIANS 13:12 NIV

Have you ever heard of the "Bubble Boy"? Born in 1971 with severe combined immunodeficiency (SCID), David Vetter had to live his entire life, from birth to age twelve, isolated in a sterile plastic environment at the hospital where he was born and then in his home. In 1976, John Travolta starred in a made-for-TV movie, *The Boy in the Plastic Bubble*, based on David's life.[25]

Can you imagine what life would be like if you never touched another person? No hugs or good-night kisses. Not even a pat on the back. Even a mosquito gets a pat on the back once in a while.

After the COVID-19 outbreak showed up, touching elbows replaced handshakes. Kissing? A dastardly virus might be on those lips. And everyone out in public had their faces covered with masks. Smile with your eyes, they said. Smile with your eyes. Hello, wrinkles.

SWEET SPOONFUL

But then something curious happened. Bible sales soared as people turned to God's Word for hope. Families did things together. And believers found new ways to do church and share the love of Christ, with or without hazmat suits. Believers found a way because Jesus truly *is* the way, the truth, and the life (John 14:6).

The only time
people dislike gossip
is when you
gossip about them.

–Will Rogers

Talk Is Cheap

Rumors are dainty morsels that sink deep into one's heart.
PROVERBS 18:8 NLT

"Spilling the tea" is a southern way to say sharing the latest
gossip. Hearsays spread on beautiful verandas, on front
stoops, in coffee shops, or over the phone—anywhere anyone
can run their mouth. And some folks' mouths run like a
boardinghouse toilet. When people get together, as one
southern lady put it, "We talk about nothing and a whole
lotta somethings."

The Bible describes gossip like savoring tasty tidbits
of food swallowed into the innermost parts of our body. And
it is true. When someone says they have something to tell
us about someone else, we sit still and listen as they dish the
dirt. If only we used such hyper-listening skills in church.
Men think women are the only ones who gossip, but men
enjoy hearing the latest scuttlebutt too. There is an old saying
that still rings true: "Great minds discuss ideas; average
minds discuss events; small minds discuss people."

SWEET SPOONFUL

Reckless tittle-tattle never ends well. Someone almost always
gets hurt by the untamed tongue. Once tales and scandals
are shared, the lies take on a life of their own. Babble
merchants will whisper for years to come about whatever
they hear, and the subject of the gossip and their families will
suffer the hurt and repercussions of such small talk. Gossip
is the devil's music. Don't be his DJ.

Money doesn't
change men;
it merely
unmasks them.

–Henry Ford

38

Good Teacher

When the young man heard that saying,
he went away sorrowful, for he had great possessions.
MATTHEW 19:22 NKJV

The rich young ruler who came to Jesus knew there was
something missing in his life. "What good thing shall I do
that I may have eternal life?" he asked (v. 16). Jesus told him
to keep the commandments. "Which ones?" the young ruler
inquired (v. 18).

Jesus could easily have said, "Duh, all of them." But
instead, Jesus named the commandments that apply to a
person's relationship to others. Don't murder. Don't commit
adultery. Don't bear false witness. Honor your father and
mother. Love your neighbor as yourself (vv. 18–19).

For a hot second, the young man likely thought, *Aced
it!* However, even with his superficial understanding of the
law, he knew there was something he still lacked. He didn't
understand that God gave us the law to reveal to us a standard
that is impossible for any of us to achieve without his grace.

SWEET SPOONFUL

Jesus could have rolled his eyes at this point, but he didn't.
Instead, he told the rich young man, "If you want to be
perfect, go, sell what you have and give to the poor…and
come, follow Me" (v. 21). The young man's heart drooped.
Jesus had seen straight to his heart, that money was his idol.
The young man bowed his head and went away sorrowful. He
did his best to follow the rules, but he could not follow Jesus.

Mosquitoes are
like family.
They are annoying,
but they carry
your blood.

39

Brambleberries

Those things which proceed out of the mouth come forth
from the heart; and they defile the man.

MATTHEW 15:18 KJV

We all have someone in our family circle who acts like
they've been weaned on a pickle. Cantankerous. Friendly as
a bramblebush. Tough as a stewed skunk. Sister Sandpaper
or Brother Hammer. They rub everyone the wrong way any
chance they get. Other than avoiding them, what else can
you do around such an unpleasant person? Find the source
of their sour attitude, that's what.

Everybody has a story. Instead of allowing grouchy
people to push you away, stay and converse instead. Ask
them how they're doing and then listen to them. You will
likely be surprised by things you never knew about them.
Invest your time with this "unloved one." A bitter person
might harbor a wound to the heart that was never healed.
Of course, this technique might not work with everyone.
However, if all you manage to do is listen and share God's
love, perhaps that is all that is needed.

SWEET SPOONFUL

Jesus comes to each of our hearts in different ways. He draws
us with cords of love. Some are so afraid of being hurt again
that their hearts are surrounded by thorns. But the Lord
knows how to get past the brambles to the sweetness of
the berry. Keep loving and keep praying with patience and
perseverance. God is working in ways you cannot yet see.

Our world is filled with fear, hate, lust, greed, war, and utter despair. Surely the Second Coming of Jesus Christ...is the only hope for replacing these depressing features with trust, love, universal peace, and prosperity.

–Billy Graham

40

Herald

"To him was given dominion and glory and a kingdom,
that all peoples, nations, and languages should serve him."
DANIEL 7:14 ESV

In ancient times, trumpets were used primarily for military
marches and as signaling devices. Trumpets announced
that a king or ruler was about to make a move. The sound
of a trumpet also alerted and warned people that something
important was about to take place.

At a time yet to come, trumpets will announce that
God is about to do something big. While believers disagree
on the timing, the rapture of the saints will occur with a
shout, the voice of an archangel, and the sound of a trumpet
(1 Thessalonians 4:13–17). We will meet him in the air
and later return with Jesus Christ to the earth in triumph
(Revelation 19:14) over all the works of the Enemy.

SWEET SPOONFUL

In the book of Revelation, chapters eight through eleven,
there are seven trumpets sounded by seven angels, each
signaling separate apocalyptic events, judgments upon the
earth. But the seventh trumpet is different. The seventh
trumpet is a herald, a signal of the long-awaited arrival of
the King. This day is longed for by the faithful and dreaded
by the faithless. The end of the world as we know it is an
astonishing and glorious event in God's timeline, unveiling a
new heaven and a new earth and the biggest family reunion
that will ever be.

The fishermen know
that the sea is dangerous
and the storm terrible,
but they have never
found these dangers
sufficient reason for
remaining ashore.

–Vincent van Gogh

41

Shipshape

If I take the wings of the morning and dwell in the uttermost
parts of the sea, even there your hand shall lead me,
and your right hand shall hold me.

PSALM 139:9–10 ESV

A ship is safe and snug in a harbor, but that's not where
ships belong. They belong out at sea, where they were built
to be. Some of us were created to be missionaries or pastors.
God created others to be doctors, scientists, engineers, and
politicians. Some are writers, artists, or musicians. Whatever
you are, whatever you do, whether you are a butcher, baker,
or candlestick maker, a believer is first and foremost an
ambassador of Christ.

Every follower of Christ is commissioned by Jesus to
share the gospel with others. You might go no farther than
your own backyard fence to talk to a neighbor, or you may
very well sail the seas to a distant shore. Wherever God
sends you, let the name of Jesus be on your lips.

SWEET SPOONFUL

For fellowship to happen, you need to get to know the fellows
on the ship. It's comfortable to stick with the people you
know and quite uncomfortable to step outside that circle into
a world that does not recognize or honor the God you serve.
But the next stranger you meet could become your brother
or sister in Christ. The gospel you lovingly share might be
ignored by some yet be words of life to someone else.

On Christ the
solid rock I stand;
all other ground
is sinking sand.

–Edward Mote,
"My Hope Is Built on Nothing Less"

42

Shifting Sands

The stone that the builders rejected
has become the cornerstone.
PSALM 118:22 ESV

If you love the beach life, any day there is a blessing. Salty breezes, tousled hair, a wave-scalloped shoreline adorned with white bubble pearls can be relaxing and soothing. But venture into the water up to your ankles, and you will feel the sensation of cold sand shifting beneath your feet as the water crashes and pulls away from the shore.

Imagine what life would be like if the ground beneath your feet was constantly unstable. Safety and security would be unknown to us. There would be no hope for the future, and no true balance to count on, only living in the moment, just trying to stand. There is more to life than struggling to survive day by day. For those who reject him, Jesus is a stumbling stone and a rock of offense (1 Peter 2:8). For those who receive him, Christ is not only a rock to stand on, but he is also the chief cornerstone, a sure foundation on which to stand.

SWEET SPOONFUL

If you build your life like a sandcastle each day, all you accomplish will wash away with the evening tide. But build your life upon the rock of your salvation, and your house will stand on a sure foundation, one that will endure eternally. If you don't stand for Jesus, you'll fall for anything.

Did you hear about the notebook who married a pencil? She finally found Mr. Write.

43

Wedded Blech

"Please forgive the transgression of your maidservant; for the LORD will certainly make my lord a secure and enduring house, because my lord is fighting the battles of the LORD."

1 SAMUEL 25:28 AMP

Young women in the sixties loved playing the Mystery Date game, opening the door to either a well-put-together dream date or a sloppy dud. Of course, the game is just for giggles and grins, but Abigail was in an arranged marriage with a real dud. Her husband, Nabal, was superrich but a fool (1 Samuel 25:25).

David and his men were on the lam from King Saul and decided to protect Nabal's lambs and goats in the wilderness. When they were low on provisions, David asked Nabal for whatever he could spare. However, the man not only refused, but he also hurled insults. Not a smart move. Abigail knew she didn't have much time to act. She had the servants load up donkeys with as much nosh as she could gather and headed out to meet David before he and his men met her household with the edge of a sword.

SWEET SPOONFUL

Abigail didn't condone her husband's acts, but she made things right with David. When she told her husband, his heart failed, and he died, though Nabal's heart had truly failed him long ago. David proposed, and God disposed, and David and Abigail were married. Her first marriage was arranged, but her life suddenly changed when she took a bold step of faith.

We never know

the worth of water

till the well is dry.

–Thomas Fuller,
British scholar (1608–1661)

44

Holds Water

The wilderness and the solitary place shall be glad for them;
and the desert shall rejoice, and blossom as the rose.
ISAIAH 35:1 KJV

Succulents and cacti thrive in the arid rain shadow of the
Mojave Desert in the Southwest United States. At 120 degrees
Fahrenheit, Death Valley is the lowest and hottest portion of
the Mojave.[29] Yet some species of plants manage to survive
and thrive. The cottontop barrel cactus, grizzly-bear prickly
pear, silver cholla, and beavertail cactus grow from an
elevation of four hundred feet to the mountain summits and
survive on about two inches of rain annually.[30] Cacti store
water in their innermost succulent layer in collapsible storage
cells found in the stem or in their root system.[31]

Most of us don't live in a desert, though sometimes
we feel as if we're living in a spiritual desert, a place without
expectation. At times we feel so oppressed or depressed
we feel parched to the soul. But those who store up for
themselves a cache of living water within their innermost
parts feed their spirit with God's Word. They are prepared
and sustained both when it rains and when it doesn't.

SWEET SPOONFUL

Mojave is a word meaning "beside the water."[32] Even in a
desert, we are never far from the living water of God. And if
you ever run low, he will make a way in the wilderness and
streams in the desert (Isaiah 43:19).

Most of us can
read the writing
on the wall.
We just assume
it's addressed to
someone else.

45

Found Wanting

"This is the inscription that was written:
MENE, MENE, TEKEL, UPHARSIN."
DANIEL 5:25 NKJV

The expression "the writing on the wall," a warning of impending doom, comes from a message for Belshazzar, king of Babylon, who celebrated while his "impenetrable" city was under siege. He urged his guests to drink their wine from the captured gold and silver vessels taken from the house of God in Jerusalem. Suddenly, the fingers of a man's hand appeared and began to write on the plaster of the palace wall. (For a visual, imagine Thing from *The Addams Family*).

Shaken, Belshazzar called for an interpretation from his wise men, but only God's prophet Daniel could answer him correctly. God had weighed Belshazzar, and he came up a ninety-pound spiritual weakling. So God would divide his kingdom among the Medes and Persians (Daniel 5:25). Babylon fell that very night, and so did Belshazzar.

SWEET SPOONFUL

Author and preacher Mark Lehman Strauss wrote, "Empires do not stand by human might, man-made machines and missiles. There is not a wall high enough nor thick enough to prevent a nation from falling when God pronounces that nation's doom."[33] May we be sober and watchful and not be found wanting in God's balance.

If you want to know
how rich you are,
consider how many
things you have that
money can't buy.

46

The Green Tree

I have seen a wicked, violent man [with great power]
spreading and flaunting himself like a cedar in its native soil.
PSALM 37:35 AMP

When you're struggling to make ends meet, it's hard to see
some rich influencer waving cash around to incite people
to do evil or some flash-in-the-pan scammer making shady
bucks off the backs of hardworking people and bragging
about it. Seeing bad folks prosper is a hard pill to swallow
when you're doing your best to obey God and live a right life.

The devil tried to tempt Jesus by offering him all the
kingdoms and glory of the world if Jesus would fall down
and worship him. But Jesus answered, "You shall worship the
LORD your God, and Him only you shall serve" (Matthew
4:10 NKJV). The devil has been at this a long time. If he had
his claws in ancient kingdoms and nations, he most certainly
has his claws in modern nations today.

SWEET SPOONFUL

There are still people willing to bow down and worship the
Enemy to get what they want out of life. And all for the price
of their eternal soul. They give away their heavenly birthright
for a handful of dust and rust. Not a fair trade to be lied to by
the biggest deceiver of them all. Those who trade their souls
may rise to great heights yet lose everything in an instant.
But you know the old adage: "The higher they are, the harder
they fall."

When we work,
we work.
When we pray,
God works.

–Hudson Taylor

47

Pray-severance

Pray without ceasing.
1 THESSALONIANS 5:17 KJV

Any parent knows that children are persistent when they want something. It's called nagging. They ask the same question over and over again, hoping to wear you down. Some frustrated parents give in. Other parents send their children to a time-out to rethink their pesky ways.

But there is a Scripture passage about a man who had no food to offer to an unexpected houseguest who stopped by at midnight, so the man knocked on a friend's door to ask for three loaves of bread. His neighbor's family was asleep, yet he kept on knocking. It's hard to get out of a comfortable bed, but the man knocking was so persistent that his sleepy and plenty-annoyed friend opened the door and gave him what he asked for.

Many people would avoid bothering anyone, much less a friend so late at night. They wouldn't even ask. But this man was desperate, so he kept asking and knocking until he got what he asked for (Luke 11:5–10).

SWEET SPOONFUL

Do you pray like you're blowing wishes upon a dandelion? Sometimes God waits for the passion of our need to manifest in persistence. Don't give up until you get your answer from God. And don't knock it till you try it.

I lose patience
quicker than
I lose weight.

48

Wrong Side of Bed

The LORD is near to all who call upon Him,
to all who call upon Him in truth.
PSALM 145:18 NKJV

Some mornings you wake up with your hair looking like last year's bird nest. And everything from that moment on goes wrong. You stub your big toe right on the way to take a shower only to discover that another family member used up all the hot water. On top of that, the coffeemaker won't work. Now you're running late, so you dash out to the car, and the engine won't turn over. Just dandy.

There are times and seasons when it seems that all hades has broken loose on your life, family, health, business, even church. You feel like giving up, and you wonder where God is. *Why isn't he helping? Is he mad at me? Why isn't he on my side?*

Some people blame God and shake their fist at the ceiling in anger. But such a reaction reflects a lack of understanding about his nature and a lack of trust in his plan.

SWEET SPOONFUL

If you've asked Jesus into your heart, you are family. He will never leave you or forsake you (Hebrews 13:5–6). Your Daddy God loves you with a fierce, immutable love. When things go wrong in your life, turn to him for help, and he'll turn your circumstances into blessings.

Sometimes God lets us
hit rock bottom so
that we will discover
that He is the rock
at the bottom.

–Tony Evans

49

Rock Bottom

He drew me up from the pit of destruction,
out of the miry bog, and set my feet upon a rock,
making my steps secure.

PSALM 40:2 ESV

Pits are dark, deep, depressing places. From time to time, most of us find ourselves in a pit of despair. All anyone stuck in a hole wants to do is get out of that hole. When Joseph's jealous brothers threw him in a pit and sold him to Midianite traders, the young man was completely despondent. Betrayed by his own family, he was cut to the heart and frightened to the core.

But Joseph's darkest time was the beginning of God's refining work in Joseph's character. God raised Joseph up from serving as a slave to serving as the savior of his people (Genesis 37:12–36). Waiting is hard to do, but patiently waiting on God is a mature response honed from experience. Patience is the perfect combination of trust and control. Can you trust and wait patiently for the Lord?

SWEET SPOONFUL

Being in a pit is the pits. But you are not wasting time there when you surrender to God. The Lord will use every experience, situation, and circumstance to mold and shape your character from pride to humility, from selfishness to compassion, from a lust for revenge to openhearted forgiveness. Turn your pit into a prayer closet and see what God does.

God not only
orders our steps,
He orders our stops.

–George Müller

50

Starts and Stops

Let your eyes look directly forward,
and your gaze be straight before you.
PROVERBS 4:25 ESV

There are glorious times when we launch into a project with
what seems like a supernatural wind in our sails. Everything
goes right. All things fall into place. And life is good. But
those times are few and far between, if they come at all, for
some of us. Usually we experience pushback and conflict and
aggravations that leave us frustrated and winded.

Although it feels like you're starting and stopping
a gazillion times, you're really not stopping at all. Life is a
yardstick of notches that move us ahead by increments so
small that sometimes we have to remind ourselves that we're
still moving forward. Delays seem eternal, but so does a
time-out for a two-year-old.

SWEET SPOONFUL

All the obstacles strewn across our path, the dangers
and distractions that try to hinder us from our goals and
missions in life, are put there either by God to make us
stronger and to grow our faith or by the Enemy to try to
stop us or to slow us down. But God in his wisdom uses
whatever the Enemy meant for evil against us and turns it
into something good. God doesn't waste any opportunity
to strengthen our determination and resilience either. And
sometimes after a discouragement, there's a bit of a slingshot
effect, propelling us way ahead of where we were.

We reach God
on bended knees,
not building sprees.

51

Babbling

Just as the body is one and has many members,
and all the members of the body, though many,
are one body, so it is with Christ.

1 CORINTHIANS 12:12 ESV

The people of the land of Shinar, also known as Babylon, decided to build the tallest tower they could. United in an evil purpose, they wanted to make a name for themselves, not glorify their Creator (Genesis 11:1–4). When God showed up for a look-see, he said something interesting: "Indeed the people are one and they all have one language… Now nothing that they propose to do will be withheld from them" (v. 6 NKJV).

So God scattered the people by language and geography. Their construction led to their destruction. God dispersed the people for their ultimate good. When people join together of one accord and of one purpose, our potential and power are unlimited. When believers unite in prayer and praise, there is nothing we cannot accomplish in the name of God and for his glory. God created us to succeed *together*.

SWEET SPOONFUL

The potential for what humankind can do cooperatively for good or for evil is powerful and of eternal consequence. We cannot leapfrog our way to heaven, but heaven can reach our hearts through the love of Christ.

He came to pay
a debt he didn't owe
because we owed a debt
we couldn't pay.

52

Paid in Full

The wages of sin is death, but the free gift of God
is eternal life in Christ Jesus our Lord.
ROMANS 6:23 ESV

You know parents are always trying to pay for things. Try
to treat your parents to lunch, and your daddy will fish
his worn leather wallet out of his pocket as your mama
rummages through her suitcase-sized purse for cash before
declaring, "I got a twenty, honey!" Most parents like nothing
better than to bless their children. Even when finances
are tight, they manage to scrape enough together to buy
backpacks and new school clothes, or they work another
shift so a child can have piano lessons.

The kind of sacrificial love we see our parents
demonstrate is a beautiful reflection of Christ's love for us.
Our sin is a debt so huge that we could never gather enough
money to pay our way out of it. Mama's purse is deep but
nowhere deep enough. God loves us so much that he sent his
only Son, Jesus Christ, to pay for our sins with his own life
(John 3:16).

SWEET SPOONFUL

The blood of Jesus is rich with salvation. His blood is so
precious that no amount of paper or electronic money, or
gold, or precious metal, or bitcoin could ever come close to
reaching even a sliver of a fraction of its worth. No wealth of
any kind is worthy of the Lamb of God, yet he considered us
worth the sacrifice.

An easy way to
tell if you have
a servant heart
is how you act when
you're treated
like a servant.

–Michael F. Bird

53

Humble Pie

"Even the Son of Man did not come to be served,
but to serve, and to give his life as a ransom for many."
MARK 10:45 NIV

True stories abound of people who have inadvertently
dressed in suits or outfits that resemble the waitstaff at
weddings or in restaurants. People mistakenly signal them
over and bark orders. "Bus my table." "Top off our coffee."
"This fork is dirty. Bring me a clean one and make it snappy."
Some individuals became greatly incensed and immediately
put the offenders in their place, while others humbly do as
they are told, even wiping down the diner's tables before
quietly taking their own seat at another table. Would you like
a scoop of ice cream with that humble pie?

At the Last Supper, Jesus wrapped a towel around his
waist and washed the feet of his disciples (John 13:3–5). He
was about to lay down his life for all humanity, yet he did the
work of the lowliest of servants. The apostles must have been
beyond humbled that their master would do such a thing.
"But Lord, you don't know where my feet have been!"

SWEET SPOONFUL

To be a servant of Christ is to truly follow in his footsteps.
Jesus washed the filth of our sins away with his own precious
blood and laid down his life to redeem us from death, hell,
and the grave. He knows where we've been and what we've
done, and he still loves us.

No one ever
made a difference
by being like
everyone else.

–P. T. Barnum

54

Fun House

God said, "Let us make man in our image, after our likeness."
GENESIS 1:26 ESV

If you've ever visited a carnival fun house or house of
mirrors, you've seen images of yourself in distorted and
often humorous ways. Short and squat. Long and stretchy.
Your best and worst features magnified. Carnival fun houses
are favorite movie tropes, using a maze of mirrors—some
normal, some distorted and warped—and other frames that
only appear to be mirrors when in fact they are clear glass
through which mirrors are reflected. Nothing is as it seems.
Following your senses won't get you out of the mirror maze
because normal rules don't apply.

Sometimes we don't need a fun house mirror to see
ourselves in distorted ways. We tend to compare the way we
look to the way other people look, especially people on TV
or social media—perfectly dressed and coifed and staged,
airbrushed and multifiltered images of perfection. Such
comparison is the thief of joy, not a true reflection of the
character of God in you.

SWEET SPOONFUL

When God looks at you, he sees his unique and wonderful
creation. He looks through the exterior of who you are,
straight to your heart. Does he see the precious blood of his
Son, Jesus Christ, covering you? We are made in God's own
image and likeness, but the blood of Jesus completes us. You
once lived in sin, but now you live in him.

You have brains
in your head.
You have feet
in your shoes.
You can steer
yourself any
direction you choose.

–Dr. Seuss

55

The Trouble with Trouble

God is our refuge and strength,
a very present help in trouble.
PSALM 46:1 ESV

Some of life's troubles are those we walk hand in hand with, bad decisions that lead us to ruin and regret. The trouble with trouble is that it often starts out as fun or adventurous and maybe even a little dangerous. Some see taking a sin detour as a break from the daily monotony of being a "boring" Goody Two-shoes. A bad boy or bad girl reputation brings on a temporary popularity boost among the worldly-minded.

How does a sin detour start? With one sin at a time. Give way to sin, and sin will make a way. The Enemy's goal is to destroy you, to make you feel ashamed and unworthy to ask God for forgiveness and help. But God will not turn his ear from anyone who calls upon him. He is always willing to forgive and set us back on the right path.

SWEET SPOONFUL

Sin will take you far away from all you know and care about, to places you wish you hadn't gone, and to people you wish you had never met. There are many who wish that they had stayed, not strayed from the straight and narrow, because sin exacted too high a price. But our comfort is in knowing that when we turn to Jesus, our ever-present help, he will help us out of whatever situation we're in.

When birds burp,
it must taste
like bugs.

–Calvin to Hobbes

56

Almighty Amnesia

"I will be merciful toward their iniquities,
and I will remember their sins no more."
HEBREWS 8:12 ESV

Have you ever wondered about the above Scripture verse? Is it possible that God, who knows absolutely everything about everyone, can actually forget our sins? When we forgive someone who has wronged us, in spite of our best efforts, the hurt often lingers, marinates, and eventually ferments in the back of our minds. We distrust the person and fear they will wrong us again. "Fool me once, shame on you. Fool me twice, shame on me." But this is not so with God. When we truly repent of our sins, he will never revisit or bring them up again. "You will cast all our sins into the depths of the sea" (Micah 7:19).

God's response is often quite unlike ours. We seem to delight in belching up the past and slinging accusations at one another instead of emulating God's gracious and tender act of complete forgiveness. If we have a selective memory about our sins instead of repenting of them as we are called to do, we can be certain that God will not forget. He remembers and records our actions and even our thoughts to the tiniest detail. Unrepentant sinners will be called into account for their sins.

SWEET SPOONFUL

The choice is ours to make. God will either cast sins into a sea of forgetfulness or cast the sinner into the pit.

The Greeks had a race in their Olympic games that was unique. The winner was not the runner who finished first. It was the runner who finished with his torch still lit. I want to run all the way with the flame of my torch still lit for Him.

–Joseph Stowell,
author and past president of Moody Bible Institute

57

Carry the Light

"Keep watch, because you do not know the day or the hour."
MATTHEW 25:13 NIV

Old Testament wedding traditions were threefold, beginning with the engagement and including the betrothal and then the actual marriage ceremony. The groom and his procession would arrive unexpectedly for the bride. The bride had to be ready. No time to wash off that Queen Helene mint julep masque! Matthew 25 gives us a picture, starting at verse 1. "At that time the kingdom of heaven will be like ten virgins who took their lamps and went out to meet the bridegroom." The bride and five of her virgins were ready for the groom to arrive. The first five are the prepared kind of bridesmaids who carry extra bobby pins and tissues on them. Their lamps were lit, and they even had extra jars of oil.

But not the other five hot messes. These girls had lamps but no oil. Maybe they placed an order with Amazon. Too late. When the bridegroom showed up at midnight, they couldn't find their way to the banqueting hall. The foolish five were locked out. There seemed to be no difference among the ten bridesmaids until the defining moment. Oil represents the Holy Spirit and the people of God working together as one (Zechariah 4:1–7).

SWEET SPOONFUL

Jesus is the Bridegroom of the church, his bride, and he will arrive when we least expect him, perhaps even the midnight hour. Are you ready? Is your lamp lit?

Some people will
sell you a dream
and deliver
a nightmare.

58

There Was a Crooked Man

No one who practices deceit shall dwell in my house;
no one who utters lies shall continue before my eyes.
PSALM 101:7 ESV

Can you remember the first time an email from a mysterious stranger claiming to be a faraway prince showed up in your inbox with the offer of a lifetime? The poor royal can't take his fortune out of the country without your help. All you have to do is fork over your bank account info, and he'll deposit his money in your account for safekeeping *plus* leave you a generous monetary thank-you for your help. You might have thought, *Oh joy, today is my lucky day!* But you're about to say bye-bye to your hard-earned savings account.

Scammers like that steal your self-esteem, peace, well-being, and prosperity. Some people have had their whole life savings drained by faceless crooks across the globe. If an offer sounds too good to be true, it's probably too good to be true. Don't trust everything you see. Even salt looks like sugar from a distance.

SWEET SPOONFUL

Get-rich-quick schemes are just that—schemes to separate you from your money—and the person who gets rich isn't going to be you. Some phone or internet scams are set up to scare you into handing over your money. Trust in the Lord at all times but take what scheming strangers say with a grain of salt. Or sugar.

Some wish to live within
the sound of a chapel bell;
I wish to run a rescue
mission within a yard
of hell.

–C. T. Studd

59

Andronicus and Junia

Greet Andronicus and Junia, my fellow Jews who have been in prison with me. They are outstanding among the apostles, and they were in Christ before I was.

ROMANS 16:7 NIV

The apostle Paul makes mention of this godly couple in Romans, but little is known of them. In the Eastern Orthodox church, Andronicus is known as "Andronicus of Pannonia." Pannonia was an ancient Roman province where the two likely served. Andronicus and Junia were Paul's kin, meaning most likely the two were fellow Jews who followed Christ. They became believers sometime after Pentecost, long before Paul himself was converted on the Damascus road.[39]

Were they husband and wife? Siblings? One thing is certain. They were fellow prisoners, according to Paul, who were thrown into prison for the sake of the gospel. Andronicus and Junia were well-thought-of and had impeccable reputations among the apostles. Wouldn't all of us desire to have reputations like that? How many people would say something like that about you?

SWEET SPOONFUL

The two believers were hard workers, traveling missionaries who led many to Christ. Some claim that they were apostles, a matter best decided by Bible scholars. What is important is that they were known as fellow laborers in Christ. If that is all the historical information anyone will ever know, it is enough.

Prayer doesn't change things. God changes things in answer to prayer.

–John Calvin

60

Handy Hankies

God worked unusual miracles by the hands of Paul, so that even handkerchiefs or aprons were brought from his body to the sick, and the diseases left them and the evil spirits went out of them.

ACTS 19:11–12 NKJV

Some televangelists exploit these Scripture verses by selling special healing prayer cloths and such. Right or wrong, it's between them and God. If you don't like the fruit, walk on by the tree. God can work miracles any way he chooses to. He certainly did through the apostle Paul in his ministry and, believe it or not, through the man's handkerchiefs and aprons. People were healed and set free.

We're not talking about your grandma's church hankie either. The word used for "handkerchief" translates to "sweatband," which brings to mind an eighties workout video. These were the rags Paul wore around his head or tied around his waist when he was tent making. Maybe it all started when someone took a souvenir cloth and brought it to a sick person, and they were healed. Who knows? God will meet us wherever we are.

SWEET SPOONFUL

Whatever Paul thought about people swiping his stinky sweatbands, he couldn't argue with the results. God can reach anyone anywhere any way he chooses.

I've read the last page
of the Bible.
It's all going to
turn out all right.

–Billy Graham

61

Anteroom Antichrist

Here is wisdom. Let him who has understanding calculate
the number of the beast, for it is the number of a man:
His number is 666.
REVELATION 13:18 NKJV

God the Father alone knows the beginning of the end of the
age. We can look around at current events and try to predict,
but no one can be certain. The devil doesn't know either,
which is why he always has an antichrist waiting in the wings.

For example, the great-grandson of Noah was
named Nimrod, which means, "He who made all the people
rebellious against God." Tower of Babel ring a bell? Antiochus
Epiphanes, a hellish Hellenistic king, persecuted the Jews
and defiled God's house by erecting a statue of Zeus and
sacrificing a pig on the altar of incense. The Roman emperor
Nero Caesar was as evil as can be, persecuting and martyring
the saints relentlessly. Emperor Titus of Rome destroyed
Jerusalem and the temple in AD 70. There are more.
Alexander the Great. Napoleon. Hitler. All inexplicably rose
to power and had an insatiable hunger for conquest.

SWEET SPOONFUL

Nero's name, when translated from Greek to Hebrew, has a
numeric equivalent to 666,[41] but he was not the Antichrist.
Neither were the others. They were all forerunners of the
man of sin, the evil one who will blaspheme God, oppress
believers, and cause the whole world to bow down and
worship the beast.

Whosoever will reign with Christ in heaven, must have Christ reigning in him on earth.

–John Wesley

62

The Cross and the Throne

Jesus told his disciples, "If anyone would come after me,
let him deny himself and take up his cross and follow me."

MATTHEW 16:24 ESV

American pastor A. W. Tozer said, "In every Christian's heart
there is a cross and a throne, and the Christian is on the
throne till he puts himself on the cross; if he refuses the cross
he remains on the throne."[42] Is this a metric of the backsliding
and worldliness among gospel believers today? We want to be
saved, but we insist that Christ do all the dying.

The Bible is quite clear on this. "If we died with
Christ, we believe that we will also live with him" (Romans
6:8 NIV). Dying to self means dying to selfishness,
arrogance, and worldliness. We cannot follow Christ if we're
sitting around twiddling our thumbs. We are meant to carry
God's Word, not sit on thrones this side of heaven.

SWEET SPOONFUL

People who sit on thrones while talking on their phones will
never know the joy of serving others. They will never see
the smile on a child's face when their parents hand them a
Christmas present the parents could barely afford. Or the
tears in an elderly man's eyes at the sight of a home-cooked
meal. Or the gratitude on the face of a woman who is
homeless as she receives a warm blanket over her shoulders.
Whatever we give to others we receive back in joy. God fills
our hearts as we empty them.

We cannot force someone
to hear a message they
are not ready to receive.
But we must never
underestimate the power
of planting a seed.

63

Well Rooted

"Still other seeds fell on fertile soil, and they produced
a crop that was thirty, sixty, and even a hundred times
as much as had been planted!"

MATTHEW 13:8 NLT

If you've ever taken a boat tour along the river walk in San
Antonio, Texas, you've likely heard of or seen the famed fig
tree growing out of a limestone wall. A seed took root in a
tiny crack and inexplicably grew multiple trunks to a great
size. There are also stories of lemon and lime trees growing
from the citrus that people toss from beverages.

The parable of the sower is all about seeds (Matthew
13:1–23). Seeds that fall along the road are people who hear
the Word, but the Enemy snatches away the seeds before
they get a chance to sprout. The stony-place seedling is a
hyper-happy believer at first, but troubles come along, and
their faith fizzles. The thorny seedling is surrounded by
worldly temptations that envelop them and prevent them
from growing and bearing fruit. The parable of the sower
reads like it's all about seeds, but it's really about us.

SWEET SPOONFUL

Some believers prove to be quite hardy regardless of their
circumstance. The only reason they grow and thrive is
because they are well rooted in Christ. Are you growing
in Christ? If you aren't, then you are losing ground. Read
your Bible daily. God's Word is the living water you need to
mature and later bear fruit in the kingdom of God.

Promise only what
you can deliver.
Then deliver more
than you promise.

64

All in a Day's Work

Do you see a man who excels in his work?
He will stand before kings.
PROVERBS 22:29 NKJV

Attitude is what sets people apart. Joseph, the favored son of Jacob, couldn't have imagined he'd be betrayed by his own brothers and sold as a slave in Egypt. But he was the type of person who took seriously whatever job he was given, no matter the circumstance, and the Lord blessed him. Joseph worked diligently for his master, Potiphar, and his master soon made him the overseer of his house and all that he owned. If the boss's wife hadn't tried to go all hotsy-totsy after him, Joseph would have had continued success.

Thrown into prison for Mrs. Potiphar's false accusations, Joseph could have given in to depression. After all, his family had rejected him. He was sold as a slave and then accused of a heinous crime of which he was innocent. But Joseph poured himself into his work, and the warden noticed and put him in charge of the other prisoners. This ultimately led to Joseph's next gig as second in line to Pharaoh.

SWEET SPOONFUL

Are you giving your very best to whatever job you're called to do? The work you do now might not be what you dreamed of doing, but God may have purposed the position for you as a training ground for a future situation. When you do your work as unto the Lord and excel in all that you accomplish, you will stand before kings.

It is only rest in God's
presence and grace
that will make you
a joyful and
patient parent.

–Paul David Tripp

65

Covered with Cheese

Train up a child in the way he should go:
and when he is old, he will not depart from it.
PROVERBS 22:6 KJV

There is a rite of passage for every baby, one that involves a
high chair and a melamine bowl of chopped-up spaghetti.
We all know how it goes. More spaghetti and meatballs
will end up on that little one's head and face than will ever
make it into their mouth. And parents will take pictures,
photographs that will evoke good-natured laughter and
fun memories. And sometimes the iconic spaghetti photos
resurface when brides and grooms do slideshows at their
rehearsal dinners.

Our parents teach us many things, from language, to
the basics of the alphabet and mathematics, to good manners
and etiquette, proper hygiene, and Bible stories. Good
parents also show us how to love and be loved.

SWEET SPOONFUL

Building wonderful memories together, teaching life
skills and applications, and laying a foundation of faith
for our children are parental responsibilities most of us
take seriously. The way we parent our children is the way
we represent God as our heavenly parent. Their early
understanding of him is based on our love for God and our
walk before him. Before your little ones grow up and roll out
the door like runaway meatballs, give them an extra hug or
two and tell them how much you love them.

I love people
who make me forget
that I'm shy.

66

Shrinking Violets

God gave us a spirit not of fear
but of power and love and self-control.
2 TIMOTHY 1:7 ESV

The term *shrinking violet* refers to shy, introverted people, bashful and unassuming folks who work quietly in the background without demanding attention. Everybody knows someone who fits that description. There's the kid who hides in the shadow of his mama's apron and grows up to be a quiet guy who melts into a hedge at outdoor barbecues. There's the wallflower woman who sits on the sidelines of every group conversation, silently sipping her lemonade.

We often overlook and underrate shy people. They are great listeners because they are not flapping their jaws all the time. And they are thinkers who sometimes wish they had the nerve to speak up and set straight the people who are talking nonsense. Timid people notice things that other people don't, like an expression of hurt or sadness on someone else's face. A quiet person might be a dreamer, an artist, or (gulp) a serial killer. You never know. Their cards are definitely not on the table, but they might be complex souls with elevated thoughts and low volumes.

SWEET SPOONFUL

Maybe the only thing that separates a shy person from an outgoing person is a lack of confidence. Be that person who takes the time to get to know a shrinking violet. You never know. A beautiful friendship might bloom.

The greatest kindness one
can render to any man
consists in leading him
from error to truth.

–Thomas Aquinas

67

Hush Puppies and Such

Abraham hastened into the tent unto Sarah, and said,
Make ready quickly three measures of fine meal, knead it,
and make cakes upon the hearth.
GENESIS 18:6 KJV

The humble hush puppy is an over-the-top delicious food
that a home cook with an iron skillet can make out of almost
nothing in no time flat. Is there anything tastier than fried balls
of cornmeal dough? Golden brown and crispy on the outside,
soft, warm, and savory on the inside. The basic ingredients of
hush puppies include cornmeal, buttermilk, eggs, salt, baking
powder, grated onion, and a touch of sugar. To some, adding
any other ingredient is pure sacrilege, but there are many
variations, nonetheless. And they're almost all good.

The basic ingredients for salvation are as follows:
admit you are a sinner and repent of your sins (Romans
3:23), believe that Jesus paid the price for your sins with his
own life on the cross (John 3:16), accept that Jesus died and
was resurrected, and confess that Jesus is Lord of your life
(Romans 10:9).

SWEET SPOONFUL

There are different ways believers come to Christ, including
by altar call, a cry to Jesus for help, a deathbed confession,
and more. God is not surprised by when or how we receive
him. He prepares our hearts and sends faithful believers to
share the gospel. He gives us the ingredients. The choice of
what to make of them is up to us.

The confession
of evil works
is the first beginning
of good works.

—Augustine of Hippo

68

Signet, Cord, and Staff

"Out of the heart come evil thoughts, murders,
acts of adultery, other immoral sexual acts, thefts,
false testimonies, and slanderous statements."
MATTHEW 15:19 NASB

Judah, the older brother who sold Joseph into slavery, put
the past behind him, or so he thought. His first son married
Tamar (Genesis 38), but he died. Tamar married Judah's
second son, and he died as well. So Judah asked Tamar to
wait until his third son, Shelah, grew up, but when Shelah
reached marriageable age, Judah hesitated, fearful that
Shelah would die too.

So Tamar came up with a bold plan to ensure she
would have legal heirs and a secure future. She ditched her
widow's clothes, veiled her face, and gussied herself up like
a roadside prostitute. Judah fell for it and promised a young
goat for the attention of an old one. As surety, Tamar asked
Judah for his signet, his cord, and his staff. Three months
later, Judah found out Tamar was pregnant and called for her
to be burned for immorality…until she sent him his signet,
his cord, and his staff as proof that he was the father.

SWEET SPOONFUL

Judah's signet, cord, and staff were symbols of his identity
and character. Perhaps Judah did not like what he saw about
himself, for years later, he pledged his own life as surety for
Benjamin in Egypt. And from Perez, his firstborn twin, came
the true redemption of the world, Jesus Christ.

Optimist:
someone who figures
that taking a step
backward after taking
a step forward is not
a disaster, it's a cha-cha.

–Robert Brault,
American writer

69

Chin Up, Buttercup

"This is what the LORD says: 'You know if a man falls down,
he gets up again. And if a man goes the wrong way,
he turns around and comes back.'"
JEREMIAH 8:4 ERV

Failure may not be an option for some of us, but it happens
anyway. Defeat is easy to achieve if we don't try. But if we try
as hard as we can to succeed, at least we will know that we
gave it everything. Success is not built on success; it is built on
a foundation of failures. You will only truly fail if you give up.

Every time you lose at something, you hopefully learn
from what went wrong until you do something to make it
right. Failure helps us find a hundred or even a thousand ways
something won't work. All we need to find is the one way that
does. And with God's help, we can see our way to success.
"Nothing will be impossible with God" (Luke 1:37 ESV).

SWEET SPOONFUL

Failure is not always an outcome we have control over, but
giving up is something we can control. Setbacks can be
disheartening and downright depressing. We can feel like
throwing in the towel. But when we ask God for inspiration,
fresh ideas, and new ways of looking at things, he nudges
and guides us to the solution for our problem or hindrance.
And he helps us in other unexpected and miraculous ways.

The world is
your oyster.
It's up to YOU
to find the pearls.

–Chris Gardner,
American businessman and
author of *The Pursuit of Happyness*

70

The World Is Your Oyster

"In the world you will have tribulation;
but be of good cheer, I have overcome the world."
JOHN 16:33 NKJV

Jonathan Swift is credited with saying, "He was a bold man who first ate an oyster." Have you ever wondered what prompted a person to try the first slimy, shiny, gray, squishy, and cold snot glob of goodness? Somebody tried 'em and liked 'em, bless their heart.

Some believe that pearls form in an oyster from a particle of grit in its shell. But the truth is that naturally occurring pearls form around an irritating parasite, like a sea worm or egg. To protect itself from harm, the oyster encases such parasites in nacre, a lustrous material also known as mother-of-pearl.

When the Enemy worms his way into our lives, he means to injure or destroy us, rendering us incapable of serving God. But believers have the wonder-working power of the blood of Jesus with which to defeat him. Layering Scripture, prayers, and trust in God onto our pain and suffering transforms them into objects of beauty before the Lord.

SWEET SPOONFUL

The Enemy thinks the world is his oyster, but he was defeated by Christ on the cross. Satan is an irritating parasite, a pretender to the throne, and a liar who deceives. God has given us all the tools we need to shuck the Enemy of his deception and cast the empty shell of lies away.

Desire not to
live long but well.
How long you live,
not years but
actions, tell.

71

Old Friends

If they fall, one will lift up his fellow. But woe to him who is alone when he falls and has not another to lift him up!
ECCLESIASTES 4:10 ESV

If you know friends long enough, they truly become old friends. You pat one another on the back or hug 'em hello and tell folks, "I've known this guy since Moby was a guppy." Old friends have certain characteristics you just can't get from new ones. You have a history, especially if you have known one another since childhood. Maybe you swiped an apple pie or two off a windowsill together. Or were chased by a bull as the two of you crossed a field.

Old friends are broken in. You've had all the scraps you're ever going to have. Fights so bad you raised hell and stuck a chunk under it. Old friends share memories and remember for one another when one forgets. Finishing one another's sentences is an act of love. You share secrets, but you'll never tell anyone he has false teeth, and he'll never tell anyone you comb over your hair. Finally, old friends are loyal. If someone says something about your pal, the back of your neck bristles. "Hush that fuss before I put up my dukes!"

SWEET SPOONFUL

Author H. Jackson Brown Jr. said, "Remember that life's most valuable antiques are dear old friends."[46] New friends are a blessing from God, but there's nothing like an old one.

Fresh food from
the farmer's market
is all well and good
until a cricket climbs
out of your salad.

72

Bounty of the Earth

"Look! I have given you the seed-bearing plants throughout
the earth and all the fruit trees for your food."
GENESIS 1:29 TLB

Home gardening is a "growing" pastime, gaining in popularity
for a variety of reasons. People like fresh food from heirloom
plants, untainted and untreated, not genetically modified, and
without pesticides. Our grandparents and great-grandparents
grew their own vegetables and herbs in victory gardens
during the two world wars and in kitchen gardens before that.
They maintained fruit and nut trees and "put up" peach jam
and apple butter. They handpicked huckleberries, dewberries,
blueberries, strawberries, and raspberries, and they went
blackberry picking with a big stick in one hand to poke at
snakes.

Whatever you grew in the season, you ate, and you
canned the rest to eat later. For families who want to eat
healthy food, the opportunities are out there. God has given
us what we need to grow and thrive.

SWEET SPOONFUL

After they were cast out of the garden of Eden, Adam and
Eve became gardeners themselves. Things didn't grow east
of Eden as easily as they did in Eden. But they learned to
till the earth, care for their crops, and enjoy what the earth
produced. You can produce fruit for the kingdom of God the
same way, with hard work, diligence, and patience.

Medieval thoughts:
Roses are red.
Violets are blue.
And neither are
useful or necessary.

73

Height of Romance

With all humility and gentleness, with patience, bearing with one another in love, eager to maintain the unity of the Spirit in the bond of peace.

EPHESIANS 4:2–3 ESV

Romance during the Middle Ages looked and sounded a lot different. Modern women like heartfelt cards, costly bouquets, candlelit dinners with champagne, and, hopefully, some kind of fancy chocolate dessert. In medieval times, marriage for women of means meant a union of power and alliance with other wealthy families. "Will you become my wife so that I can take all your dowry money and own you as my personal possession for the rest of your life?"

Rich men married to gain sons, not hearts. Some peasants actually got to marry for love and affection, but peasant life was hard. "Will you marry me so we can farm crops, raise livestock, and possibly starve together in the winter?"

Is it a coincidence that the first two words in *medieval* are *me* and *die*? Lots of people died at an early age of the plague and other diseases and afflictions.

SWEET SPOONFUL

Modern times are a whole lotta not perfect, but more people have a better quality of life than anybody had in the Middle Ages. Jesus came to give us life and life more abundantly (John 10:10). Be thankful for the quality of life he has blessed us with and that people nowadays like to bathe.

In the sweet by-and-by,
we shall meet on that
beautiful shore.

–Sanford Fillmore Bennett,
"In the Sweet By-and-By"

74

Sweet By-and-By

"Give, and it will be given to you. Good measure, pressed
down, shaken together, running over, will be put into your lap.
For with the measure you use it will be measured back to you."

LUKE 6:38 ESV

There's a saying among financial planners that goes "You
can either give with a warm hand or a cold hand." If you're
blessed with money, give to your loved ones and charities
while you're still around or give after you're under the
ground. Our motto during our working years is often to get
all we can, can all we get, and then sit on the can. Most of us
are not really saving the money for ourselves but to pass it on
to our children after we're in the sweet by-and-by.

But we should feel free to enjoy some of the fruits
of our labor during our golden years. Travel as it suits
your fancy. Enjoy time with family and friends. Spend,
give some away, and keep enough aside to live your life in
a comfortable yet modest fashion. The legacy you give to
churches, charities, and children will make a difference in
so many lives. That's something nice to see while you're still
around to see it.

SWEET SPOONFUL

Our money represents our time on this earth. We get paid
by the hour. Before you clock out, use your time and money
wisely to bless others and to further God's kingdom, and you
will pass down an eternal inheritance.

If you're a Christian,
your search for approval
should be over.

–David Jeremiah

75

Over Yonder

As high as the heavens are above the earth,
so great is His mercy toward those who fear Him.
PSALM 103:11 NASB

Everyone knows someone who lives out in the boonies,
places where GPS is not likely to work. They live so far out
in the country that the sun sets between their house and
town. Directions to their homestead include lines like, "Go
left at the railroad crossing with the Goats for Sale sign next
to the tracks, keep driving a piece till you cross over Gibson's
Gulch, then hang a hard right down the dirt road with the
lucky horseshoe nailed to a sassafras tree next to it, and
then you're only a hoot and a holler away." Only friends and
family who really love and care about them ever answer the
invitation to visit. Getting there is a sacrifice of love.

SWEET SPOONFUL

The good news is we don't have to travel far at all to find
Jesus. He keeps his eyes on us, lovingly waiting for that one
special day, that one particular, glorious moment when you
fall to your knees and ask him into your heart to be your
Lord and Savior. Heaven celebrates. A choir of angels sings
joyful praise. When you rise, your heart is lighter, and the
sun shines a little brighter. Before salvation, we feel like God
is far away, but he is always close by, waiting for us to answer
the invitation.

God never uses
anyone greatly
unless he tests
them deeply.

—A. W. Tozer

76

Better Call Paul

"The time is coming when those who kill you
will think they are doing a holy service for God."

JOHN 16:2 NLT

Before he was the apostle Paul, he was a smarty-pants
religious scholar, Saul, who had a murderous desire for the
lives of those who followed Christ. With the approval of the
high priest, he called for Christians to be stoned to death. And
he was such a nice guy that he kept an eye on people's cloaks
while others did the stoning. Saul was fully convinced he was
following God's law and will and that God approved of what
he was doing. That is, until one day on the road to Damascus,
Jesus knocked Saul off his high horse and said to him, "Saul,
Saul, why are you persecuting Me?" (Acts 9:4 NKJV).

Whoever persecutes God's children persecutes Jesus
himself. When God's heavenly light encompassed him, the
first thing Saul asked was "Who are You, Lord?…What do
You want me to do?" (vv. 5–6). Saul, whose name means
"question," asked Jesus what most new believers ask, and the
Lord guided him one step at a time to his new life.

SWEET SPOONFUL

Jesus knew what was going on in Saul's heart. Perhaps the
heart change began when Saul presided over the stoning of
Stephen (Acts 7:57–60), and he heard Stephen's beautiful
prayer of forgiveness as he lay dying. Saul was also called
Paul, which means "humble," one piece of evidence among
many that he had become a new creature in Christ.

Discernment is not knowing the difference between right and wrong. It is knowing the difference between right and almost right.

–Charles Spurgeon

77

Behind the Facade

Beloved, believe not every spirit, but try the spirits
whether they are of God: because many false prophets
are gone out into the world.

1 JOHN 4:1 KJV

Why are some believers so dense when it comes to
discernment? Your boss hires a no-account ne'er-do-well.
And you just shake your head and think, *Even the chickens
under the porch could have picked someone better.* Your
church brings someone on staff who has horns holding up
his fake halo. Your child has a friend who is a bad influence.
There are some folks who don't know a widget from a
whangdoodle. And why is that?

Evangelist Smith Wigglesworth said, "To discern spirits
we must dwell with Him who is holy, and He will give the
revelation and unveil the mask of satanic power on all lines."[49]
Spending time with God in prayer, immersing yourself in
his Word, and waiting on God until he answers is the way
to spiritual perception. Discernment is seeing things with
God's eyes. Our own eyes deceive us. We look at the outer,
superficial appearance, but God looks straight to the heart.

SWEET SPOONFUL

One thing to keep in mind about discernment is that our
greatest strength stands next to our greatest weakness. There
is a temptation to judge instead of to pray and tell the truth
in love. Discernment won't do anyone any good if we reveal
it in the wrong spirit.

Need an ark?

I Noah guy.

78

Lonely Petunias

If the world hate you,
ye know that it hated me before it hated you.
JOHN 15:18 KJV

Noah was called by God to build an ark. He preached to the evil and corrupt people of the earth for 120 years. Instead of a repentant response to the call to righteousness, Noah's neighbors mocked and ridiculed him. In fact, as far as we know, he was the only preacher without a single convert (2 Peter 2:5). When the first drops of rain began to fall, Noah and his family boarded the ark, and God himself shut the door tight.

Do you ever feel like a lonely little petunia in an onion patch? If you're the only one in your family or group of friends who is a believer or has moral, social, or political opinions different from the rest, you probably sometimes feel disheartened and discouraged. People we love and care about can be callous and hurtful at times.

SWEET SPOONFUL

Do your opinions and beliefs line up with God's Word? Some people can interpret Scripture ten ways from Sunday, but that doesn't mean they are right. The world and the Word are incompatible. Pray and stand your ground with quiet and humble fortitude. Say what you mean, mean what you say, but don't say it mean. Speak the truth in love even if others don't love you back.

Be respectful even to
nasty hateful people
because your mama
raised you better.

79

Art of Graciousness

Offer hospitality to one another without grumbling.
1 PETER 4:9 NIV

In this day and age when people cuss the alphabet like they breathe, it's nice to hearken back to a time when, beginning at an early age, many parents taught their children to consider what came out of their mouths. Genteel folks conversed with others in a decent, respectful way. Polite conversation always included speaking *and* listening. People shied away from making spectacles of themselves. Events like that could tarnish the family's name, and back then, a family name used to mean something.

Mothers often taught their children that, if they couldn't say something nice about somebody, they should say nothing. They practiced polite ways of offering their opinions, too, like "Common sense is a flower that doesn't grow in everyone's garden." People sent thank-you notes for gifts and birthday cards in thoughtful remembrance. Visitors felt comfortable in a gracious and hospitable home. "Please" and "thank you" were expected. No one would ever dare disrespect their elders. And if someone you knew was under the weather, you would bring them a casserole.

SWEET SPOONFUL

Thankfully, gracious living is not a lost art. You can be an example of graciousness to others. People will notice something different about you, and maybe they will dare to be different too.

We are immortal
until our work
on earth is done.

–George Whitefield

80

The Two Swords

The weapons of our warfare are not of the flesh
but have divine power to destroy strongholds.
2 CORINTHIANS 10:4 ESV

Jesus had told his disciples that he was about to be rejected
and crucified (Luke 18:31–33). So they were fearful and
decided to weapon up with a couple of swords. One can
only imagine the gentle disappointment on Jesus' face. He
had sent them out two by two to heal the sick and cast out
demons (Matthew 10:1), yet now they feared for their lives.

When Judas showed up at the garden of Gethsemane
with between three hundred and six hundred soldiers to
arrest Jesus, Simon Peter drew his sword and sliced off the
ear of the high priest's servant (26:51). Jesus reached out
and touched the wound, restoring the ear instantly. "'Put
away your sword,' Jesus told him. 'Those who use the sword
will die by the sword'" (v. 52 NLT). The disciples began to
understand that their truest weapon was his Word.

SWEET SPOONFUL

After Christ's resurrection, the disciples understood Christ's
power over death, hell, and the grave. And they no longer
feared death. Most of them were later martyred in a variety
of unpleasant ways. Yet they shared the gospel openly,
lovingly, and at all times, even with their last breath. They
loved more than they feared.

If you were
not strangers here,
the hounds of the world
would not bark at you.

–Samuel Rutherford

81

Lambs with Teeth

"Whatever you ask in prayer, you will receive,
if you have faith."
MATTHEW 21:22 ESV

Do you know soldier saints who suit up with the armor
of God daily and tear down enemy strongholds prayer by
prayer? Maybe you are one of them. But there are others who
are content to stand on the sidelines, offering milquetoast
monologues that tickle the ears and prayers with no teeth.

Some believers think that if they don't mess with
the devil, then he won't mess with them. But he attacks all
Christians because the Enemy of God is also the Enemy of
humankind. The devil hates God, and he especially hates
us because we are made in God's image. We are his beloved
sons and daughters, favored, called, and chosen. If you are
not a threat to the Enemy, you should be.

SWEET SPOONFUL

We are to be as "wise as serpents and innocent as doves"
(Matthew 10:16). The devil is a shrewd player, deceitful in
every way, and evil to the core. But the boundless wisdom of
God is beyond that of a serpent or any other created thing.
The saints of God are pure, washed in the blood of Jesus,
white and innocent as little lambs on the outside. But we are
filled and imbued with the overcoming power of his blood.
When the Enemy comes close, open your mouth and pray.
Show the Enemy your spiritual teeth. Believers are lambs
with teeth, outwardly gentle yet fierce and faithful for God.

The water met
its Master
and blushed.

–Lord Byron

82

Whine Not

"Everyone brings out the choice wine first and then the cheaper wine after the guests have had too much to drink; but you have saved the best till now."

JOHN 2:10 NIV

Families in the Old Testament planned and approached weddings with a deep sense of reverence, as sacred and eternal covenants with God. People in little Podunk towns couldn't afford to put on fancy weddings, but they did the best they could. The wedding in Cana (John 2:1–11) was no exception, but the most embarrassing thing happened— the hosts ran out of wine, and the wedding guests were beginning to whine about it. So Mary asked Jesus if he would do something about the situation.

Mary knew her son and knew that he could and would do something to help. Jesus instructed the servants to fill six large purification pots with water and then draw some out and take it to the master of the banquet, a sort of ancient times wedding coordinator. One sip of the wine wowed the guy, and he asked the bridegroom why he had served the two-buck chuck at the beginning of the wedding feast and saved the vintage wine for last.

SWEET SPOONFUL

Jesus has saved the best for last for us with the new covenant of grace. The law revealed our propensity for sin and its consequences, but the new covenant of grace forgives our sin debt. For believers, the best is yet to come.

Only the deepest love
will persuade me
into matrimony,
which is why I shall
end up an old maid.

–Elizabeth Bennet,
Pride and Prejudice (2005 film)

83

Cakes Cry Tiers

Being confident of this very thing,
that He who has begun a good work in you
will complete it until the day of Jesus Christ.

PHILIPPIANS 1:6 NKJV

Ever heard of a cake pull? Unless your wedding is in New
Orleans, probably not. The tradition goes back to Victorian
times. Eligible females circle the wedding cake to pull a
ribbon from the bottom tier. Each ribbon is tied to a charm,
and each charm has a meaning. The ring charm is the most
desired because the woman who pulls it is supposed to be
the next bride. A horseshoe or four-leaf clover indicates
good luck. A telephone charm is a wish for good news. The
anchor means hope. The heart, impending love.

But a button or the thimble means the girl will be an
old maid. Heaven forbid! And if the old maid label isn't bad
enough, the girl who pulls a penny charm is in for a life of
poverty.[51]

No one really believes that pulling a silver charm
from a cake will forecast their future. But some folks go from
simple tradition to superstition. They want to know what's
ahead. Trouble is, they go to the wrong source.

SWEET SPOONFUL

Your life is in God's hands. If you want to know about your
future, go to your Creator. "I know the plans I have for you,
declares the LORD, plans for welfare and not for evil, to give
you a future and a hope" (Jeremiah 29:11 ESV).

Any bad day
can be fixed
by driving a
backcountry road
with the
radio up and
the windows down.

84

Far From

Devote yourselves to prayer
with an alert mind and a thankful heart.
COLOSSIANS 4:2 NLT

If you're tired of doomscrolling and commenting on social media all day, there's a reason for that. An onslaught of mean-spirited posts and comments and images can cause us mental and emotional anguish.

Jesus was always surrounded by crowds hemming in on him. He loved and desired to help everyone, but after a while, he needed a break. "Jesus often withdrew to lonely places and prayed" (Luke 5:16 NIV). Christ set an example for us to follow.

We all need to renew our minds in the presence of the Lord. In a world dominated by a sea of voices and talking heads spouting opinions, threats, and curses, we need to withdraw from those who cackle and clamor and instead seek out personal times of peace and refreshment. Never miss an opportunity to shut up and shut down.

SWEET SPOONFUL

Charles R. Swindoll said, "Tell yourself right now and throughout today, that it's okay to draw away from the maddening crowd. Jesus did it; so can you."[52] God did not create us to take in the volumes of news and information we bombard our minds with daily. Only God is equipped to take that on. Instead of keeping your eyes glued to a scrolling screen day and night, turn your eyes toward Jesus.

Passing on a spiritual heritage to your children takes more than simply teaching God's Word; it takes *living out* God's Word. Fathers and mothers become a picture of Jesus to their children.

–Pastor Jack Hibbs

85

Half-Baked

Children, obey your parents in everything,
for this pleases the Lord.
COLOSSIANS 3:20 ESV

If you had a deal with your kids to pay them allowance
money for mowing the lawn but saw that they mowed only
half of it, would you still give them the money? Absolutely
not. A half-done job is not a completed job.

Yet there are believers who think that God should give
them credit for good intentions rather than actions. They
think, *I was going to give that homeless person some money, but
I don't carry cash anymore. I would have held the door open for
that man on crutches, but I was late for a meeting.* They say the
road to hell is paved with good intentions, and perhaps that's
true. The Lord honors obedience, not lip service.

SWEET SPOONFUL

Unfortunately, some parents *would* give their kids an
allowance for half-done chores, and they're doing their
children a disservice. Those kids will go through life
thinking that they receive a reward no matter what kind of
effort they put in.

Without self-awareness or introspection, that attitude,
lack of respect for authority, and poor work ethic will carry
on throughout their lives and affect their spiritual life too.
Those who don't respect natural authority won't respect
supernatural authority.

Hope is the thing
with feathers
That perches in the soul,
And sings the tune
without the words,
And never stops at all.

–Emily Dickinson

86

Feather Crowns

He will cover you with his feathers,
and under his wings you will find refuge;
his faithfulness will be your shield and rampart.

PSALM 91:4 NIV

"Every tub must stand on its own bottom," as Paul Bunyan
wrote in *Pilgrim's Progress*. So it's natural to wonder whether
some departed loved ones made it through the pearly gates.

In certain parts of the Ozarks and Appalachia,
folklore about "feather crowns" persists. The crowns, found
in the pillows of those who have died, look something like a
"bun" of feathers woven together naturally. Superstition says
such a crown indicates the deceased has gone to heaven.

Could these crowns have formed naturally through
daily use of the feather pillow? Probably. But then again,
maybe not. When a loved one passes, family members eagerly
probe the pillows of the deceased, hoping to pluck out one of
these curious creations. Curiously enough, feather crowns are
sometimes found in the pillows of people who lived, *ahem*,
rather colorful lives. Perhaps for some relatives, a fabricated
crown is sometimes all they can do to save face.

SWEET SPOONFUL

The good news is that believers don't have to wonder
whether they have a feather crown. A real crown of
righteousness awaits us in heaven (2 Timothy 4:8).

One leak will
sink a ship;
and one sin will
destroy a sinner.

–John Bunyan

87

Gone to the Dogs

Submit yourselves therefore to God.
Resist the devil, and he will flee from you.
JAMES 4:7 ESV

"A Native American elder once described his own inner
struggles in this manner: 'Inside of me there are two dogs.
One of the dogs is mean and evil. The other dog is good.
The mean dog fights the good dog all the time.' When asked
which dog wins, he reflected for a moment and replied, 'The
one I feed the most.'"[54]

What a beautiful description of the battle going
on inside each of us! The apostle Paul described his own
inner struggles in this way: "I do not understand my own
actions. For I do not do what I want, but I do the very thing
I hate" (Romans 7:15). Believers have a renewed spirit but a
rebellious body.

SWEET SPOONFUL

The desire to sin is always with us in varying degrees, but the
more we resist it and turn to God, the less hold that sin has
over us. Humble yourself before God first. This is the order
of authority in the kingdom of God. Submit that sin to God,
for he opposes the proud but shows favor to the humble
(James 4:6). When we are submitted to God, our sin is also
under God's authority, and we have supernatural power to
resist temptation. Let your desire for God be greater than
your desire for sin. Which dog are *you* feeding the most?

How sweet is rest
after fatigue!
How sweet will
heaven be when our
journey is ended.

–George Whitefield

88

Sea of Glass

I saw what appeared to be a sea of glass mingled with fire—
and also those who had conquered the beast and its image
and the number of its name, standing beside the sea of glass
with harps of God in their hands.

REVELATION 15:2 ESV

The Grand Canyon Skywalk at Eagle Point in Arizona is a
horseshoe-shaped, transparent walkway that extends seventy
feet out over the rim of the canyon. Visitors standing on the
platform, composed of five layers of specialized glass, can see
thousands of feet down to the canyon floor. That's enough to
make you curl up like a pill bug!

But can you imagine standing beside a vast,
bottomless sea of glass in heaven? Is this lucid, luminous
sea merely part of the architecture of heaven? Some
commentators say that this heavenly sea might instead be
the physical representation of the Word of God, connecting
the idea of the Old Testament tabernacle's laver and the New
Testament washing of water by the Word (Ephesians 5:26).
The glass represents God's transparency toward us. And the
fire, God's holy judgment. God's Word likewise cleanses and
transforms us.

SWEET SPOONFUL

Deep water rises and billows, ever waving toward shores,
but the sea of glass is peaceful and serene before the throne
of the living God. For believers, heaven is our tranquil
destination and forever home.

If I were Snow White,
you'd never be able to
kill me with an apple.
You'd have to poison an
éclair or something.

89

For What Ails You

"They will be able to handle snakes with safety,
and if they drink anything poisonous, it won't hurt them."
MARK 16:18 NLT

Jesus commanded his disciples to go out into all the world and preach the gospel, cast out demons, speak with new tongues, heal the sick, and…take up serpents? Drink poison? Okay, first part sounds good, but let's circle back to that part about snakes and poison.

Paul was bitten by a viper (Acts 28:3) and was miraculously unharmed, but what if this passage is more significant to modern times? Our air, water, food, homes, workplaces, and the soil in which plants grow are poisoned with chemicals, pesticides, and various toxins. Our food and water supplies contain chemical and radioactive waste, heavy metals, and pathogens. Bacteria and viruses transmit life-threatening illnesses.

Perhaps God is both warning and reassuring us to pray for healing, deliverance, and protection over ourselves and our loved ones. We are "fearfully and wonderfully made" (Psalm 139:14 KJV). Our bodies are strong and resilient, made in God's image. Pray God's Word over the venoms and poisons of this world.

SWEET SPOONFUL

Though the viper's venom should have killed Paul, it had no effect on him. "No weapon formed against you shall prosper" (Isaiah 54:17 BSB).

In a postapocalyptic
situation,
instead of looking for
a survival shelter,
I would look for an
Amazon warehouse.

90

Doomsday Devotions

"Surely I am with you always, to the very end of the age."
MATTHEW 28:20 NIV

There are questions that keep turning up like a bad penny. Questions you never think anyone would ask these days, but they do. Is the earth flat? Will I fall off if I keep walking? Are Sasquatches lurking around campgrounds waiting for an opportunity to steal beef jerky? Are reptilians secretly taking over the world?

While we can't be sure about the last two questions, we can be sure that if the earth were flat, cats would have pushed everything off it by now. Better not to worry about things that might occur or could theoretically happen. Like nuclear war. Biological weapons. Zombies. Fire tornados. Earthquakes. Hurricanes. Skynet. God already told us how things are going to turn out. We don't need any other narrative to look to. History is "his story," and we haven't gotten to the final chapter yet.

SWEET SPOONFUL

Worrying about what might happen won't do any of us a lick of good. The philosopher Michel de Montaigne (1533–1592) is believed to have quipped, "My life has been full of terrible misfortunes, most of which never happened." Funny thing, we worry more about the scenarios we conjure up in our imagination than the truth written in the book of Revelation. The day of the Lord is a blessing for believers but a true doomsday to those who reject God.

Endnotes

1   *Merrie Melodies*, "Leghorn Swoggled," written by Warren Foster, directed by Robert McKimson, aired July 28, 1951.

2   *Merrie Melodies*, "Of Rice and Hen," written by Warren Foster, directed by Robert McKimson, aired November 14, 1953.

3   Hyman J. Appelman, "I Know There Is a Heaven," in *God's Answer to Man's Sin* (Grand Rapids, MI: Zondervan, 1940), available online at https://www.baptistbiblebelievers.com/LinkClick.aspx?fileticket=lyjn EU4Lmj8%3d&tabid=388&mid=1245.

    Epigraph, 3: Lewis Grizzard, *They Tore out My Heart and Stomped That Sucker Flat* (Montgomery, AL: NewSouth Books, 2010), 38.

    Epigraph, 6: Joey Adams, *Cindy and I: The Hilarious Adventures of Mr. and Mrs. Joey Adams* (New York: Popular Library, 1959), 6.

    Epigraph, 8: Greg Laurie, "Beyond These Shadowlands," in *Every Day with Jesus: Forty Years of Favorite Devotions* (Lake Mary, FL: Charisma House, 2018), 211.

    Epigraph, 12: Max Lucado, *And the Angels Were Silent: The Final Week of Jesus* (Nashville, TN: Thomas Nelson, 2013), 71.

8   Lauren Cahn, "19 Funniest Tombstones That Really Exist," *Reader's Digest*, February 15, 2023, https://www.rd.com/list/funniest-tombstones-that-really-exist/.

9   "This Date in History: June 14, 2007—Remembering Ruth Bell Graham," The Billy Graham Library, June 14, 2012, https://billygrahamlibrary.org/this-date-in-history-june-14-2007-remembering-ruth-bell-graham/.

Epigraph, 15: Billy Graham, "The Door Is Still Open," *Decision*, February 1, 2023, https://decisionmagazine.com/billy-graham-the-door-is-still-open/.

11 Justine Tal Goldberg, "200 Million Americans Want to Publish Books, but Can They?" Publishing Perspectives, May 26, 2011, https://publishingperspectives.com/2011/05/200-million-americans-want-to-publish-books/.

Epigraph, 20: *The Chronicles of Narnia: The Voyage of the Dawn Treader*, directed by Michael Apted (2010, Los Angeles: 20th Century Fox, 2011), DVD, 113 min.

13 Frederick William Robertson, "The New Commandment of Love to One Another," sermon, October 20, 1850, Frederick W. Robertson (website), http://www.fwrobertson.org/sermons/ser16.htm.

14 *The Vance Havner Quotebook: Sparkling Gems from the Most Quoted Preacher in America*, ed. Dennis J. Hester (Grand Rapids, MI: Baker Publishing Group, 1986), 137.

Epigraph, 25: Leonard Ravenhill, "Weeping between the Porch and the Altar: Part 2," sermon, 1994, Lindale, TX, Ravenhill (website), http://www.ravenhill.org/weeping2.htm.

Epigraph, 28: John Piper, *Don't Waste Your Life* (Wheaton, IL: Crossway, 2003), 35.

17 Tom Fanshawe, "Eyam and 'the Last Great Visitation,'" Data Mine, October 2012, https://rss.onlinelibrary.wiley.com/doi/pdf/10.1111/j.1740-9713.2012.00608.x.

Epigraph, 29: Lady Bird Johnson and Carlton B. Lees, *Wildflowers across America* (New York: Abbeville Press, 1988), 264.

19 Justin Butts, "The Spirit of Lady Bird," *The Bend*, March 29, 2019, https://www.thebendmag.com/the-spirit-of-lady-bird/.

Epigraph, 30: Rodney Dangerfield, *It's Not Easy Bein' Me* (New York: HarperCollins, 2009), 93.

Epigraph, 31: Charles Stanley, "Life Principle 14: God Acts on Our Behalf," TV sermon, In Touch Ministries, November 1, 2019, Brightcove Player, 45:13, https://www.intouch.org/watch/sermons/life-principle-14-god-acts-on-our-behalf.

Epigraph, 33: Tim Tebow, *Shaken: Discovering Your True Identity in the Midst of Life's Storms* (New York: Crown Publishing Group, 2018), 29.

23 Vince Havner, *When God Breaks Through: Sermons on Revival* (Grand Rapids, MI: Kregel Academic Publishing, 2003), 44.

Epigraph, 34: Ann Voskamp, *One Thousand Gifts: A Dare to Live Fully Right Where You Are* (Grand Rapids, MI: Zondervan, 2010), 15.

25 Shannon Quinn, "The Real Bubble Boy Helped Cure a Rare Disorder," History Collection, October 29, 2018, https://historycollection.com/the-real-bubble-boy-helped-cure-a-rare-disorder/.

Epigraph, 37: Herbert V. Prochnow, *The New Speaker's Treasury of Wit and Wisdom* (New York: Harper and Row, 1958), 190.

Epigraph, 38: Henry Ford, "It Would Be Fun to Start Over Again," interview by Bruce Barton, *The American Magazine*, 91, no. 4 (April 1921): 124.

Epigraph, 40: Billy Graham, "Introduction" in *Re-Entry II* by John Wesley White (Fenton, MI: Mott Media, 1985), 8.

29 "Death Valley: Weather," National Park Service, accessed on March 12, 2023, https://www.nps.gov/deva/learn/nature/weather-and-climate.htm.

30 "Death Valley: Cacti and Desert Succulents," National Park Service, accessed on March 12, 2023, https://www.nps.gov/deva/learn/nature/cacti.htm.

31 "Where Cactus Store Water to Survive in Deserts," Cactusway, accessed on March 12, 2023, https://cactusway.com/where-cactus-store-water-to-survive-in-deserts/.

32 "The Name Mojave," Mojave Desert Heritage and Cultural Association, accessed on March 12, 2023, https://mdhca.org/the-name-mojave.

33 Mark Lehman Strauss, *The Prophecies of Daniel* (Neptune, NJ: Loizeaux Brothers, 1969), 168.

Epigraph, 49: Tony Evans, *The Power of Knowing God* (Eugene, OR: Harvest House Publishers, 2020), 29.

Epigraph, 53: Michael F. Bird, *Romans*, The Story of God Bible Commentary, eds. Tremper Longman III and Scot McKnight (Grand Rapids, MI: Zondervan, 2016), 427.

Epigraph, 55: Dr. Seuss, *Oh, the Places You'll Go!* (New York: Random House Children's Books, 1990), 2.

Epigraph, 56: Bill Watterson, *The Complete Calvin and Hobbes*, Book Three (Kansas City, MO: Andrew McMeel Publishing, 2006), 390.

Epigraph, 59: Norman Percy Grubb, *C. T. Studd, Athlete and Pioneer* (Atlantic City, NJ: World-Wide Revival Prayer Movement, 1947), 170.

39 Wikipedia, s.v. "Andronicus of Pannonia," last modified on May 20, 2022, https://en.wikipedia.org/wiki/Andronicus_of_Pannonia.

Epigraph, 61: David Poling, *Why Billy Graham?* (Santa Fe, NM: Sunstone Press, 2007), 109.

41 Michal Hunt, "The Gematria of the Number of the Beast—666," Agape Bible Study, accessed on March 15, 2023, https://www.agapebiblestudy.com/charts/Gemetria%20and%20the%20Number%20of%20the%20Beast%20666.htm.

42 A. W. Tozer, *The Radical Cross: Living the Passion of Christ* (Camp Hill, PA: WingSpread Publishers, 2009), 155.

Epigraph, 65: Paul David Tripp, "You Don't Need More Parenting Advice," Desiring God, October 8, 2016, https://www.desiringgod.org/articles/you-dont-need-more-parenting-advice.

Epigraph, 69: Robert Brault, *Round Up the Usual Suspects* (Scotts Valley, CA: CreateSpace Independent Publishing, 2014), 140.

Epigraph, 70: Chris Gardner (@CEOofHappYness), "The world is your oyster," Twitter, May 24, 2017, 6:15 p.m., https://twitter.com/CEOofHappYness/status/867519357966065664.

46 H. Jackson Brown Jr., *Life's Instructions for Wisdom, Success, and Happiness* (Nashville, TN: Thomas Nelson, 2000), 79.

Epigraph, 75: David Jeremiah, *Your Daily Journey with God: 365 Daily Devotionals* (Carol Stream, IL: Tyndale House Publishers, 2016), 261.

Epigraph, 76: A. W. Tozer, *The Root of the Righteous* (Chicago: Moody Press, 2015), 165, Kindle.

49 Smith Wigglesworth, *Greater Works: Experiencing God's Power* (New Kensington, PA: Whitaker House, 1999), 374.

Epigraph, 83: *Pride and Prejudice*, directed by Joe Wright (Hollywood: Universal Studios, 2005), 127 min.

51 "Charmed: History of Cake Pulls," Joe Gambino's Bakery, accessed on March 16, 2023, https://gambinos.com/new-orleans-history/charmed-history-cake-pulls/.

52 Charles R. Swindoll, *Day by Day with Charles Swindoll* (Nashville, TN: Thomas Nelson, 2000), 222.

Epigraph, 85: Jack Hibbs, Lisa Hibbs, and Kurt Bruner, *Turnaround at Home: Giving a Stronger Spiritual Legacy Than You Received* (Ontario, Canada: David C. Cook, 2013), 29.

54 Eliot Jay Rosen, *Experiencing the Soul: Before Birth, during Life, and after Death* (Jawahar Nagar, Delhi: Motilal Banarsidass Publishers, 2006), 15.

About the Author

Linda Kozar is an award-winning author of multiple fiction and nonfiction inspirational books, among them *Sweet Tea for the Soul* (ECPA Bronze Sales Award 2022) and *Sunshine for the Soul* (Blue Ridge Mountains Christian Writers Conference Selah Award in the devotionals category and Nonfiction Book of the Year 2021). Linda was named American Christian Fiction Writers Mentor of the Year and has been involved in her local chapter since its inception. She and her husband, Michael, live in The Woodlands, Texas, and enjoy spending time with their two grown daughters; wonderful son-in-law; grandchildren, Eden and Wesley; and Gypsy, their rascally Jack Russell terrier. Learn more about Linda at lindakozar.com.